MONTESQUIEU

QUID SECUNDATUS POLITICAE SCIENTIAE INSTITUENDAE CONTULERIT

by

EMILE DURKHEIM

Edited, with a commentary, by W. Watts Miller
Translated by W. Watts Miller and Emma Griffiths

DURKHEIM PRESS

OXFORD

© **Durkheim Press Ltd 1997**

First published in 1997 by Durkheim Press Ltd
PO Box 889, Oxford OX2 6GP

A CIP record for this book is available from
the British Library

ISBN 09-529936-00

CONTENTS

To Etienne Halphen and Bill Pickering

PREFACE

Montesquieu's *Spirit of the Laws,* published in 1748, is one of the outstanding works of modern social thought. Durkheim's Latin thesis, published in 1892, is one of the outstanding interpretations of that work, but also a seminal statement of his own views.

It is hoped that this new edition of the thesis will be of value to anyone with an interest, generally, in modern social thought, as well as to specialists on Montesquieu and on Durkheim.

It is the first direct English translation from the Latin text, and at the same time includes the Latin text itself, which has been long out of print. It also includes a relevant yet relatively unknown piece by Durkheim on Taine.

This preface deals with various preliminary points. A broader, interpretive essay follows, after the texts themselves.

A first, technical point is that the thesis page numbers and page breaks are the same as in the original edition. So are Durkheim's own notes, which appear as footnotes and as originally numbered. Editorial notes appear separately, as endnotes, and are lettered.

The English translation faces the Latin, on similarly numbered pages (but with an additional "e" – e.g., "7e", "8e", etc. – and with the omission of the blank pages – 10 and 70 – separating the introduction and conclusion from the main chapters). The translation runs in parallel, more or less, with the original text, so that the English page breaks also occur, more or less, as in the original text. An

advantage of this is that in almost all cases a reference to the thesis can be a single reference, with the same page number covering the original Latin edition, the new Latin edition and the new English translation.

Another advantage, of course, is that it is easier in reading the English to relate it to the Latin, or, as with Durkheim's many footnote quotations from Montesquieu, to the French. Making it easier to do this has also been a reason for not attempting a very free translation, but for sticking with one that is more literal and conventional.

Drafts of an English translation and of a corrected and annotated edition of the original text were prepared by W. Watts Miller, as a "Durkheimian". These were gone over by Emma Griffiths, as a classicist. And, after discussions with one another, a final version emerged. We also consulted earlier translations – Alengry's, into French, published in 1937, from a manuscript done in the 1890s and shown to Durkheim himself; Cuvillier's, into French, published in 1953; and Manheim's English translation of Cuvillier's French edition, published in 1960.

But it has made a difference to our approach that our translation, unlike the others, is side by side with the original text. It has been another reason for sticking, as translators, with the the more literal and conventional, and leaving radical interpretive decisions to readers themselves. This has involved, amongst other things, preserving ambiguities in the original text, rather than trying to resolve them – a vice, if we see it as that, of Alengry as well as of Cuvillier, and, following him, Manheim. It has also involved annotated corrections to the original text, and the most important case is where a passage is straightforward and makes complete sense, but only on the assumption that a "not" has been left out (p. 68, note a).

Most of the time, however, matters are relatively unproblematic, and this is so with many of Durkheim's key terms – such as *societas* ("society"), *populus* ("people") and *civitas* ("state"), which, indeed, he often seems to use interchangeably (e.g., p. 25, note 1). It is true that, though he repeatedly and happily uses the noun, *societas*, it is only very rarely that he uses the adjective, *socialis* (p. 37, note a). But in its stead he often uses *civilis* – as in *civilia facta*, translated here as "social facts".

Emphasis on Durkheim's talk of and concern with *societas*, *civilia facta* and their study takes us to what is perhaps the main problem of translation-cum-interpretation. He sometimes mentions *sociologia* (pp. 7, 66). He never mentions a *scientia socialis* (let alone a *scientia civilis*). He nearly always talks of *scientia politica* and its study of *res politicae* – which, for reasons already explained, our translation leaves as *political* science and *political* things. But does he really mean *social* science, and *social* things?

Alengry and Cuvillier both opt for this more radically interpretive translation, and they may well be right. It is not just that Durkheim's other work – including his main thesis, in French, on the division of labour – is clearly concerned with social science and its study of social facts and social things. It is also that in the Latin thesis itself the opening list of *res politicae* consists, not only of laws, but of morality, religion, etc. (p. 11), while one of its main arguments is that Montesquieu develops a classification, not simply of governments, but of societies (ch. 3), and another is that "he opened the way to his successors who, in inaugurating *sociology*, did not do much more than bestow, on the kind of study undertaken by him, a name" (p. 66).

So perhaps it is simply that Durkheim felt constrained, by Latin usage of the day, to translate "social science" as *scientia politica,* and then also opted, to translate "social

3

things", for the more stylish and consistent *res politicae*. My own suspicion is that he had in mind other, greater issues, or, at the least, to create mischief – by challenging the very conception of political science in vogue at the time, and by taking possession of the name in the cause of the approach and methods of sociology.

But whatever the case, and although I agree with Alengry's and Cuvillier's interpretation, that the thesis is really about social science and social things, the aim of this translation is less to impose an idea of what the text means, and more to convey an idea of what it in fact says.

A related aim is to establish the text in a critical edition, and to present it in its integrity.

Cuvillier's translation is more readily available than Alengry's, and is in general excellent. However, it replaces Durkheim's Latin translations of passages from Montesquieu with the original passages themselves, so suppressing interesting differences between them. It involves a small number of misprints and mistakes in the main text. And it reprints Durkheim's notes – which are full of mistakes – largely without correction. Manheim's English edition of Cuvillier runs into the inevitable problems of a translation of a translation, which include a reproduction, in English, of errors in the French. Nor is it always adequate as a translation of the French. And it omits most of Durkheim's notes. Nonetheless, all three translations have been invaluable in the business of turning even quite straightforward sentences around and around, in search of a reasonably accurate translation yet in reasonably acceptable English.

Changes of the original Latin text, correcting the few misprints that occur in it, are indicated in the editorial

notes. So are changes of Durkheim's footnotes, correcting the many mistaken references in them. The footnotes also contain extensive quotations from Montesquieu in French. But checking up on these is a complex matter.

It is difficult to go to the edition of *L'Esprit des Lois* that Durkheim used, since he does not cite one, and I went to the text in the only edition of Montesquieu's collected works at the time, by Laboulaye (1876-78). But where this compromises on Montesquieu's 18th century orthography and punctuation – e.g., changing *loix* to *lois,* without changing *seroit* to *serait* – Durkheim radically modernizes it. Perhaps he did this himself, working from an original edition. So I also consulted, amongst others, the facsimile of the 1758 edition produced by Masson (1950), and the recent, radically modernizing edition by Derathé (1973).

Durkheim's modernized orthography has been kept intact (and has also been used in quoting Montesquieu in my own notes). So has his punctuation, except where it departs from all three just-mentioned editions: I have then used Laboulaye in these cases (as also in my own notes). Quotation gaps unsignalled by Durkheim are reinserted in square brackets. So are bits of text accidentally left out. Corrections to mistakes – such as *principes,* instead of *principales* – are again indicated in my notes.

Durkheim submitted his main thesis, on the division of labour, in March 1892, and his subsidiary Latin thesis in November 1892. The examining jury met in 1893. It included Paul Janet, who, along with Albert Sorel, stands above other commentators at the time on Montesquieu's social and political theory. Durkheim, it will be argued, stands above them all.

W. Watts Miller

QUID SECUNDATUS POLITICAE SCIENTIAE

INSTITUENDAE CONTULERIT

MEMORIAE
FUSTEL DE COULANGES

EMILE DURKHEIM

MONTESQUIEU'S CONTRIBUTION TO THE ESTABLISHMENT OF POLITICAL SCIENCE

TO THE MEMORY OF
FUSTEL DE COULANGES

EMILE DURKHEIM

QUID SECUNDATUS SCIENTIAE POLITICAE

INSTITUENDAE CONTULERIT

PROOEMIUM

Historiae nostrae immemores, consuevimus scientiam politicam ducere alienam a moribus nostris gallicoque ingenio. Quoniam enim clarissimi philosophi qui de his rebus recentissime scripserunt in Britannia aut Germania floruere, obliti sumus hanc scientiam apud nos primum exstitisse. Attamen non modo Comte noster eam primus omnium bene fundavit, in suas partes descripsit et nomine proprio, quanquam aliquatenus barbarico, sociologiam[a] scilicet, appellavit, sed omnis ille impetus ad politicas quaestiones a philosophis nostris, qui duodevicesimo saeculo vivebant, exortus est. Ex illa autem inclyta scriptorum manu longe ante omnes eminet Secundatus[b] quippe qui in suo libro, qui *De l'Esprit des Lois* inscribitur, novae disciplinae principia instituerit.

Sane in hoc opere Secundatus non de omnibus politicis factis disseruit, sed de unico genere eorum, id est de legibus. At ratio qua ad interprentendas varias juris

MONTESQUIEU'S CONTRIBUTION TO THE

ESTABLISHMENT OF POLITICAL SCIENCE

INTRODUCTION

Unconcerned with our history, we tend to look on political science as something foreign to our ways and to the French temperament. The leading modern writers on the subject come from Britain or Germany and as a result of their success we have forgotten that this science started up in our own country. But it is not just that it was Comte who first established it on a sound basis, described its different elements and gave it its own – if somewhat barbarous – name of sociology.[a] This whole surge of interest in political enquiry originated with the *philosophes* of the eighteenth century. Amongst that brilliant group of writers, it is Montesquieu[b] who stands far above them all and who, in *The Spirit of the Laws*, laid down the principles of the new discipline.

Of course, Montesquieu did not undertake an examination of all political facts in this work, but only a particular type of these, namely, laws. Nonetheless, the method he used for understanding different forms of law

formas utitur, et ad cetera civilia instituta valet omninoque transferri potest. Immo, cum leges ad totam civilem vitam pertineant, eam fere universam necessario attingit ; nempe ut exponat quid sit domesticum jus, quomodo leges cum religione, moribus, etc., concinant, naturam familiae, religionis, morum considerare cogitur, ita ut vere tractatum de summa rerum politicarum scripserit.

Ne speres autem hunc librum sententiis abundare quae, tanquam plane demonstrata theoremata, praesenti scientiae retineri possint. Eo enim tempore, omnia paene instrumenta deerant quae necessaria sunt ut naturam civitatum penitus scrutari queamus. Historia, adhuc infans, primum adolescere incipiebat ; peregrinatorum narrationes de gentibus remotis earumque moribus et legibus rarissimae erant et incertae ; nova illa disciplina qua varii vitae eventus, mortes, matrimonia, crimina, etc., certa ratione computantur, nondum erat in usu. Praeterea, cum civitas nihil aliud sit quam immane quoddam animal quod propriam suam mentem, nostrae menti cognatam, habet, leges humanae societatis eo melius et facilius reperiuntur quo leges humanae mentis jam cognitae sunt ; novissimo autem saeculo omnia haec in initio tantum erant et vix inchoata. At procul abest quin nulla alia via de scientia bene merendi sit quam eam veritatibus certis locupletari ; sed non minoris pretii est eamdem suae materiae, naturae ac methodi consciam efficere et fundamenta quibus stabit praeparare. Illud autem est quod studiis nostris Secundatus contulit. Res gestas saepius non recte interpretatus est et ita ut facile redarguatur ; sed

also holds good for other social institutions and is of general applicability. Indeed, it is because laws relate to every aspect of social life that he necessarily touches on almost all of it. To explain the nature of domestic law, the way in which laws tie up with religion, morality, etc., he is forced to examine the nature of the family, of religion and of morality, so that he wrote, in fact, a treatise on political matters as a whole.

But we should not expect that the book is full of claims that modern science could hold on to as clearly established theories. There was a lack, at the time, of almost all the means we require for a thorough, in–depth investigation of the nature of societies. History, until then simplistic, was just beginning to develop a more mature approach. Travellers' accounts of remote peoples and their customs and religions were scant and unreliable. The new discipline, which collates different events in life – deaths, marriages, crimes, etc. – according to a definite method, was not yet in use. Moreover, the state is in a way just a vast living being with a mentality of its own, similar to ours, so that discovery of the laws of human society is easier and less uncertain when there is already knowledge of the laws of the human mind – and in the last century all this was only at an initial, difficult and tentative stage. Yet it is by no means the case that the only way to serve science is to add to its stock of settled truths. It is at least as important to make it aware of its subject matter, its nature and method, and to prepare the foundations for its development. This is the contribution that Montesquieu made to our studies. He is quite often wrong in his interpretation of history, so that is easy to contradict him.

nemo antea tam longe processerat in hac via quae posteros ad meram politicam scientiam adduxit; nemo tam plane perspexerat quae conditiones essent hujus scientiae institutioni necessariae.

Sed quae sint hae conditiones prius exponamus.

Yet no one before him had gone so far along the road which led his successors to a genuine political science. No one had seen so clearly the conditions necessary for establishing this science.

Let us first set out these conditions.

CAPUT PRIMUM

QUAE SINT CONDITIONES INSTITUTIONI POLITICAE SCIENTIAE NECESSARIAE

I

Nulla doctrina scientiae nomen meretur quae non materiam aliquam determinatam, quam exploret, habeat. Scientia enim in rebus versatur ; nisi quid ei datum sit quod describat et interpretetur, in vacuo consistit nec quicquam est quod sibi proponere possit ultra hanc descriptionem atque interpretationem.[a] Ea ratione numeros arithmetica considerat, geometria spatium et figuras, scientiae naturales corpora animata et inanimata, psychologia denique mentem humanam. Itaque ut scientia politica institui posset, ante omnia necessarium erat materiam certam ei assignari.

Primo quidem adspectu nihil promptius esse videtur quam hanc difficultatem exsolvere. Nonne enim Politica res politicas, id est leges, mores, religiones, etc., pro materia habet ? Sin autem historiam respicies, tibi constabit nullum philosophum, usque ad recentissima tempora, eas ita concepisse. Etenim omnia ea ab hominum voluntate ita pendere arbitrabantur ut eadem non sentirent vere res esse, haud secus atque ceteras naturae res, quae suas proprietates habent ideoque scientias requirunt, quibus describantur et explicentur ; sed satis esse videbatur si humanae voluntati quid petendum, quid fugiendum esset in societatibus consti-

CHAPTER ONE

THE NECESSARY CONDITIONS OF THE ESTABLISHMENT OF POLITICAL SCIENCE

I

No discipline merits the name of science that does not have a definite, limited subject matter to investigate. Science is concerned with things. Without a given to describe and explain it exists in a void and it cannot set itself any goal beyond this description and explanation.[a] Mathematics studies numbers, geometry space and figures, the natural sciences animate and inanimate bodies, and psychology, finally, the human mind. To be in a position, then, to set up and establish political science, it was above all necessary to assign it a definite subject matter.

At first sight nothing seems easier than coming up with the solution to this problem. Does not Politics study political things – that is, laws, morals, religions, etc? But if we look back into history it is clear that there have not been any philosophers, until very recently, who conceived of them in this way. They thought that these were all so dependent on the human will that they did not regard them as really things, just like other things in nature, which have their own characteristics and which therefore require sciences able to describe and explain them. It seemed enough to ask what, in the constitution of human societies, the human will should aim for or avoid.

tuendis, quaerebatur. Itaque civilia instituta et facta, non qualia essent et unde orte, sed qualia esse deberent, inquirebant ; non iis curae erat naturae imaginem quam maxime veram nobis reddere, sed ideam perfectae cujusdam societatis admirationi et imitationi nostrae proponere. Aristoteles ipse, quamvis experientiae magis quam Plato consuluerit, non communis vitae leges reperire sibi proposuit, sed quae sit optima civitatis forma. Principio ponit civitatibus nihil aliud appetendum esse quam ut cives virtutis usu felices efficiantur virtutemque in contemplatione consistere ; neque hoc statuit tanquam legem quam societates revera observent, sed observare debeant ut homines naturam suam exsequantur. Postea quidem res historicas respicit, sed fere tantum ut eas judicet monstretque quomodo sua principia variis casibus aptari possint. Alii vero politici sciptores, qui Aristoteli successerunt, hujus exemplum plus minusve secuti sunt. Seu res omnino negligunt, seu attentius aut levius eas considerant, omnes ad id pergunt, non ut eas cognoscant, sed corrigant aut etiam ab imo ad summum convertant ; praesentia igitur praeteritaque nihil paene habent quod eos detineat, [a] sed ad futurum spectant. Omnis autem doctrina, quae ad futurum spectat, cum certa omnino materia careat, non scientia, sed ars appellatur.

Fateor equidem hanc artem sine quadam scientia nunquam fuisse. Nemo enim unquam asseruit aliquam reipublicae formam ceteris anteponendam esse qui non argumentis demonstrare tentaret cur eam anteponeret ; haec autem demonstratio e rebus constet necesse est. Si quis, exempli gratia, democratiam credit aristocratiae praestare, illam cum humana natura melius congruentem monstrat, aut historia ostendit a liberis gentibus alias superatas esse, etc. Quodcumque ten-

In discussing social facts and institutions they considered, not their nature and origin, but what they ought to be. They were concerned, not with giving us as true a likeness of nature as possible, but with holding up to us, to admire and try to copy, an idea of the perfect society. Aristotle himself, although more attentive than Plato to experience, set out to discover, not the laws of collective life, but the best form of state. He assumes, from the start, that the one and only object of states is to make their citizens happy through the practice of virtue, and that virtue lies in contemplation. He does not establish this as a law which societies actually observe, but as something which they ought to observe for the fulfilment of human nature. Later, at least, he examines historical facts, but almost solely to judge them and show how his principles can fit different particular cases. Other political writers coming after Aristotle have more or less followed his example. Whether they take no notice of facts, or consider them with greater or less attention, all aim, not at a knowledge of things, but at their reform or even total transformation. Thus the present and the past have almost no interest for them. They are concerned, instead, with the future. But every doctrine concerned with the future completely lacks a definite subject matter and so is not called science, but art.

No doubt this art has always involved some sort of science. Nobody has ever claimed that a certain form of commonwealth is preferable to others without trying, with arguments, to prove why, and this has to have a basis in facts. If, for example, it is thought that democracy is better than aristocracy, it is shown that it is more in accordance with human nature, or it is demonstrated from history that free peoples overtook others, etc. Whatever it is that we attempt to do, when we use

tamus, cum ratione utimur seu ad rerum naturam scrutandam, seu ad praecepta vitae edicenda, ad res redeundum, ergo ad scientiam.

At primum, cum scriptores suas his de rebus opiniones e conditione humana potius quam e statu societatum deducere soleant, haec scientia, si modo eo nomine uti liceat, nihil quod vere politicum sit plerumque in se continet. Quid enim ? Cum demonstratum est homines ad libertatem natos esse, aut contra securitate ante omnia egere, et inde concluditur quomodo respublica constituti debeat, ubi est scientia politica ? Quidquid in iis disputationibus scientiam imitatur, ad psychologiam pertinet, quidquid autem ad politicam, ars est ; aut, si quid forte ad meram politicarum rerum descriptionem et interpretationem attinet, hoc certe minorem secundumque locum obtinet. Hujus generis est Aristotelis doctrina de causis quae constitutiones mutant aut evertunt.

Praeterea scientia, cum arte miscetur, sinceram naturam suam servare nequit, sed in nescio quid ambiguum vertitur. Ars enim, cum in actu consistat, festinare cogitur scientiamque, quam in se habet, secum rapit et urget ; scientia autem tantam festinationem non patitur. Nam quoties inquiritur quid agendum sit — quod proprium artis munus est — non cunctari sine fine licet ; sed quam promptissime respondendum est, quia vivendum. Si civitas laborat, non dubii haerere possumus dum politica scientia morbi naturam descripserit et causas repererit ; sed sine mora agendum est. Attamen, quia sumus mente praediti et deliberandi facultate, non temere decernimus ; immo, necesse est intelligamus aut potius intelligere credamus consiliorum nostrorum rationes. Itaque facta quae nobis in promptu sunt colligimus, conferimus, celeriter interpretamur ;

reason – whether to investigate nature or to lay out rules of life – we must return to things, and therefore to science.

At first, however, writers tended to derive their views on these matters from the human condition rather than from the state of societies, so that this science – if it is acceptable to apply the term to it – usually did not contain anything that is genuinely political. When it has been shown that men are born for freedom, or, on the contrary, that their overriding need is for security, and it is then concluded what the state's constitution ought to be, where, in all this, is the political science? Anything that resembles science in these disputes has to do with psychology, and anything to do with politics is art. Or if a genuine description and explanation of the political realm is somehow involved, it has a minor, secondary role. This is the case with Aristotle's theory of the causes of the change or overthrow of constitutions.

Moreover science, when mixed together with art, cannot keep its own nature intact, but turns into something quite dubious. Art is action, and so must press rapidly on, taking up and sweeping the science it contains along with it; yet science cannot be hurried in this way. Asking what is to be done – art's proper function – rules out endless delay and hesitation. It is necessary to have as quick an answer as possible, because it is necessary to live. If the state is in trouble we cannot wait around in uncertainty until political science has described the nature of the problem and discovered the causes; we must act at once. But because we possess intelligence and a power of deliberation we do not decide blindly. We must understand – or, rather, believe we understand – the reasons for our decisions. We accordingly collect, compare and quickly interpret facts that come to hand.

uno verbo, scientiam extemporalem inter eundum instituimus qua opinio nostra fundata esse videatur. Ea est scientia quae media ipsa in arte invenitur ; vides autem quam adulterata ! Propterea quod sine ulla methodo processit, nihil aliud praebere potest quam dubias probabilitates quae nullam fere auctoritatem apud nos habeant nisi quam nos ipsi iis suppeditemus. Eas enim sequimur, non quod argumenta quibus demonstrari videntur nihil incerti relinquunt, sed quia intimis affectibus nostris respondent : nos ad id tantum inclinant quod sponte expetimus. Ceterum in iis quaestionibus, cum de utilitate nostra agatur, omnia affectus animi acriter movent. Quod ad vitam nostram tanti momenti est non tranquilla mente expendere possumus ; sunt autem quae amamus, quae odimus, quae optamus, nostraque odia, amores, desideria nobiscum afferimus quae meditatitionem nostram perturbant. Adde quod nulla certa regula exstat qua quid per se utile sit, quid non, secerni possit. Nam cum plerumque una et eadem res ex una parte utilis, ex altera contra damnosa sit, neque damnum cum utilitate more mathematico comparari queat, quisque naturam suam sequitur et ex indole sua aut hanc aut illam partem unice considerat alteramque omittit. Sunt, exempli gratia, qui civium concordiae adeo student ut nihil utilius esse censeant quam si civitas quam maxime una efficiatur, nec libertatem desiderent nimia hac cohaerentia sublatam ; sunt contra qui libertatem ante omnium ponunt. Itaque totus ille argumentorum contextus, quibus variae illae sententiae nituntur, non res rerumque verum ordinem exprimit, sed animorum tantummodo habitus : quod a vera scientia abhorret.

Scientia igitur ab arte ita discrepat ut naturam suam sequi non possit, nisi juris omnino sit, id est certae

In a word, we improvise a science out of them, which seems a foundation of our opinion. This is the science encountered at the core of art itself. It can be seen how much it is debased! Since it proceeds without any method it can offer only dubious probabilities, with almost no authority for us except that which we ourselves give them. We go along with them because they correspond with our innermost feelings, and not because the arguments that seem to support and demonstrate them leave nothing uncertain. They incline us only to what we seek spontaneously. And when our interest is at stake everything arouses powerful emotions. We cannot calmly consider a matter which is so important in our life. There are things which we love, which we hate, which we desire, and we come complete with the hatreds, loves and desires which throw our thought into confusion. Add to this the lack of any sure rule to sort out what is in itself useful from what is not. It is often the case that one and the same thing is beneficial in a certain respect, but harmful in another, and since it is impossible to weigh up and compare harm, as against benefit, mathematically, everyone follows their own nature and concentrates, according to their disposition, on only this or that particular aspect while ignoring another. Some people, for example, are so keen on social harmony that what matters most for them is as united a state as possible, and they do not miss the freedom that this excessive cohesion destroys. Others, in contrast, put freedom before everything else. The entire fabric of arguments supporting these different opinions expresses neither things nor the true order of things, but only states of mind: which is the opposite of true science.

Science is thus so unlike art that it cannot follow its own nature unless it exists wholly in its own right, that is,

cuidam materiae sese applicet ut eam cognoscat, sine ulla utilitatis cura. Ea enim conditione, urgente nulla vitae necessitate, procul a forensibus privatisque certaminibus in umbratili pace et tranquillitate studiis vacare licet, nec quidquam nos incitat ut longius in concludendo progrediamur quam sinunt argumenta. Sane ea ipsa quae de rebus abstractis cogitamus e pectore oriuntur ; pectus enim fons totius vitae. Sed, ni animi affectibus temere inservire velimus, opportet eos ratione moderari rationemque ideo supra vitae casus et eventus extollere ; namque aliter, cum cupiditatibus omnigenis impar sit, se quo impellerent necessario converteret.

Ne credas autem scientiam ideo inutilem esse ad regendam hominum vitam ; arti contra eo magis auxiliatur quo melius ab ea separatur. Etenim quid nobis optabilius est quam mente et corpore sanos esse ? Sola autem scientia determinari potest in quo consistat mentis corporisque bona valetudo. Scientia enim, cum varias hominum societates per genera et species separet, quae sit normalis vitae politicae forma in quaque specie non describere non potest, propterea quod speciem ipsam describit ; nam quidquid ad speciem attinet normale est, quidquid autem normale, sanum. Praeterea cum in altera scientiae parte de morbis morborumque causis agatur, non modo quid optandum, sed etiam quid fugiendum et qua via arcenda pericula sint, admonemur. Itaque hoc artis ipsius refert ut scientia ab ea sejuncta quasi manu mittatur.

Addendum est autem cuilibet scientiae suam materiam propriam et peculiarem esse debere : nam si cum aliis scientiis eam communem haberet, ipsa cum iis confunderetur.

is applied to a definite subject matter in order to know this, without any concern with usefulness. It is on this condition that, free from any vital necessity, and away from public and private conflicts, there can be leisure to study and reflect in peace and quiet, without any pressure on us to go further in a conclusion than is warranted by the arguments. No doubt, even in abstract matters, our ideas spring from the heart; for the heart is the source of all life. But if we do not wish to be the blind slaves of passions, we must constrain them with reason and so must set reason above life's accidents and contingencies. Otherwise, unequal to desires of all kinds, it can go only where they take it.

It must not be thought from all this that science is of no help in the conduct of human life. On the contrary, it is of more use to art the better it is kept distinct from it. What is more desirable for us than to be sound in body and mind? But what constitutes good physical and mental health can be determined only by science. Science distinguishes different human societies by general class and type, and so it necessarily describes the normal form of social life in each type in describing the type itself: for whatever pertains to the type is normal, and whatever is normal is sound. And since another part of science is concerned with disease and its causes, we are informed by it, not only on what is desirable, but on what to avoid and how dangers can be prevented. So it is important for art itself that science is separated from it and, in a way, freed.

It should be added that every science must have its own specific, distinctive subject matter: if it shared this with other sciences it would be confused with them.

II

Non omnis autem materia scientiae apta est.

Scientiae primum opus est res, de quibus agitur, quales sint describere. Si vero adeo inter se differant ut nullum genus constituant, nulla earum descriptio rationali via tentari queat. Singulae enim ex se, omissis aliis, considerari ac definiri debeant. At omni individuo insitae sunt infinitae proprietates inter quas nulla selectio fieri possit ; describi autem infinitum nequit. Nihil aliud igitur reliquum esset nisi ut poetarum litteratorumque more tractentur qui res, quales esse videntur, sine ulla ratione et methodo depingunt. Contra, si in genera redigi possunt, aliquid habent quod vere definire liceat atque hoc est quod eorum naturam constituit. Nempe quae omnibus individuis ejusdem generis communia versantur, finita sunt et eorumdem essentiam declarant ; satis est igitur alia aliis superponere et qua congruant notare. Uno verbo, scientia non individua, sed genera tantum describit. Itaque prior scientiae pars nullum in Politica locum habebit, nisi societates humanae divisionem illam per genera ac species patiantur.

Aristoteles quidem aristocratiam, monarchiam atque πολιτείαν jamdudum distinxerat.[a] Ne confundas autem societatum species ac varias reipublicae formas. Duo enim populi diversorum generum esse possunt, etiamsi eodem modo gubernentur. Sic quaedam πόλεις, id est graecae civitates, et pleraeque barbarorum gentes monarchiae nomen aeque merentur et ab Aristotele[1] acceperunt propterea quod sub regibus utraeque vivebant ;

---

1. *Εἰσὶ βασιλεῖαι τῶν βαρβάρων.* (*Pol.*, III, 14, 1285 a, 17.)

II

Not everything lends itself to study by science.

A science's first task is to describe, as they are, the things with which it is concerned. However, if they differ to such an extent that they do not constitute a type it is impossible to try to describe them in a systematic, rational way. They must be examined and defined singly, in themselves and independently of the others. But each, as an individual case, incorporates an infinity of properties amongst which a selection cannot be made. And the infinite cannot be described. So nothing remains except a poetic, literary treatment, depicting, without reason and method, things as they appear. If, however, they can be reduced to types, they have something which can be genuinely defined and it is this which consitutes their nature. What all individuals of the same type have in common is finite and reveals their essence. So it is enough to compare their characteristics and see where they agree. In sum, science does not describe individuals, only types. Politics lacks a basic element of science without a division of human societies by class and type.

Aristotle, of course, long ago distinguished aristocracy, monarchy and the republic.[a] But we should not confuse types of society with different forms of state. Two peoples can be of different types, although they are governed in the same way. Some of the Greek city states and most of the foreign, "barbarian" nations could equally well be called monarchies, and are accepted as such by Aristotle,[1] because both groups lived under kings.

---

1. "[There is another form of monarchy, not uncommon in] the kingships that exist amongst foreigners." (*Pol.,* III, 14, 1285a, 17).

natura tamen differunt. Quin etiam, apud eumdem populum civitatis regimen commutari potest etsi populus ipse in aliam speciem non ideo transferatur. Ea igitur Aristotelis divisio de societatum natura nihil exprimit. Philosophi autem qui de his rebus postea scripserunt eamdem imitati sunt neque ullam aliam tentavere ; scilicet humanas societates inter se comparari posse non credebant, nisi quod ad reipublicae formam attinet. Cetera autem quae ad mores, religionem, commercium, familiam, etc., spectant, ita fortuita et inconstantia esse videbantur ut ea ad genera et species reducere nemo susceperit. Attamen ea sunt quae populorum naturae penitus inhaerent ; ea est vera politicae vitae ideoque scientiae materia.

III

At descriptio gradus infimus scientiae quae rerum interpretatione tantum absolvitur. Ad interpretationem autem aliud requiritur quod in factis politicis non minus diu inesse negatum est.

Res enim interpretari nihil aliud est quam ideas, quas de rebus habemus, ordine certo disponere qui idem sit atque ordo rerum. Quod autem hoc continet, in rebus ipsis eumdem ordinem existere, id est continuas series esse quarum partes inter se ita connectantur ut effectus quisque eamdem semper causam necessario sequatur neque ex alia oriri queat. Finge contra sublatam hujus nexus necessitatem et effectus sine causis aut e qualibet causa gigni posse, omnia extemplo fluxa et fortuita fiunt ; fluxorum autem interpretatio nulla est. Itaque eligendum est : aut res politicae scientiae repugnant aut eadem lege gubernantur qua ceterae mundi partes.

They are by nature different, nonetheless. In the same people, after all, the political regime can change completely, though they themselves do not then turn into another type. Thus Aristotle's classification of societies does not in any way bring out their nature. Yet philosophers who subsequently wrote on these questions just went along with it, making no attempt at anything different. They thought it impossible to compare human societies except through the form of state. Everything else, to do with morals, religion, commerce, the family, etc., seemed so contingent and changeable that no one tried to sort them out into kinds and types. Yet they are thoroughly bound up with the nature of societies. Here is the real matter of political life, and so of its science.

III

Description is the lowest stage of science, which is completed only by the explanation of things. But there is another condition of explanation, thought, for just as long a time, impossible to meet in the case of political facts.

To explain things is to arrange our ideas of them in a definite order, the same as the order of things. This involves the existence of such an order in things themselves – that is, the existence of unbroken chains, made up of parts which are so interlinked that every effect always follows necessarily from the same cause and cannot arise from others. Imagine, instead, that this necessary connexion is destroyed, and there can be effects without causes or that result from any cause whatever. At once, all would be ephemeral and contingent. But there is no explanation of ephemeralities. A choice must be made: either things in the political domain defy science or they are governed by the same law as the rest of the world.

Totam hanc quaestionem excutiendi non hic locus est. Monstrare tantum volumus nullam societatum scientiam esse posse si hac lege liberentur ; animadvertas autem, scientia deficiente, artem ipsam, ut vidimus, uno eodemque tempore evanescere aut certe nescio quam facultatem, praeter rationem nostram, adhibendam esse ad praecepta vitae instituenda. Ceterum, cum hoc principium, ex quo res universae arcte inter se nectuntur, in reliqua natura jam experti simus neque unquam falsum occurrerit, idem et in societatibus humanis, quae in natura continentur, valere verisimillimum est. Nihil enim rectae methodo magis contrarium est quam tot et tantas in illa regula exceptiones fingere quarum ne unum quidem exemplum novimus. Multi quidem objecerunt hanc necessitatem cum humana libertate conciliari non posse ; hanc autem disputationem, ut in alio libro jam diximus, amovere debemus.[1] Etenim, si liberum hominis arbitrium leges necessarias revera tollit, cum voluntas in rebus externis se manifestam necessario efficiat, non modo mentem, sed etiam corpus et res inanimatas omni ordine ideoque scientia expertes esse accipiendum est. At nemo est hodierno tempore qui disputare audeat num naturae scientiae institui possint ; non est cur politica scientia eodem jure non fruatur.

Homines autem et ipsi philosophi natura proni sunt ad hoc principium e rebus politicis rejiciendum. Etenim quemadmodum nullas alias actionum nostrarum rationes esse vulgo credimus nisi eas quae sub luce conscientiae voluntatem nostram videntur inclinare, ceterasque negamus esse quia eas non sentimus ; ita, in civilibus institutis, causis quae maxime conspicuae sunt vim maxi-

---

1. *De la Division du travail social,* p. I et II. [a]

18

This is not the place for a thorough examination of the issue. We wish to show only that no science of societies is possible if they are not subject to this law. And it should be emphasized that without science art itself disappears, as we have seen, at one and the same time, or must call on a strange power, beyond our reason, to lay down rules of life. Moreover, since the principle that things as a whole are closely interlinked has already been tried out in the rest of nature and never appeared false, the same is also very likely to hold good for human societies, which are part of nature. Nothing is more opposed to sound method than the supposition that this rule has so many important exceptions, when we do not know of even a single example. It is often objected, of course, that this necessity is incompatible with human freedom. But it is a dispute that, as we have already argued in another work, we ought to leave behind.[1] If human freewill really rules out necessary laws, then, since the will necessarily manifests itself in the external world, it is not only the mind but also the body and inanimate things that must be accepted as set apart from all order, and so from science. Yet there is no one nowadays ready to dispute the possibility of the natural sciences, and there is no reason why political science should not have the same status.

A natural tendency, even amongst philosophers, is to reject the principle as regards political things. We ordinarily believe that the only reasons for our actions are those whose influence on the will appears under the light of consciousness and we deny that there are others because we are unaware of them. In the case of social institutions we attribute the most force to the most obvious causes,

---

1. *The Division of Labour*, pp. i-ii. [a]

mam attribuimus, quamvis eam ex aliis accipiant : nam naturae consentaneum est ea, quae secundum cognitionem priora sunt, re quoque priora haberi. Quid autem in institutione civitatum, legum, religionum manifestius est, quid oculos magis percellit quam eorum personae qui respublicas gubernarunt, leges scripserunt, sacra edocuerunt ? Itaque regum, legislatorum, prophetarum aut sacerdotum privata voluntas totius politicae vitae fons videtur esse. Haec enim in conspectu omnium fiunt nec ullam obscuritatem in se habent. Reliqua contra, quum in secretis corporis politici partibus lateant, non facile conspici possunt. Inde nata est haec adeo vulgata superstitio ex qua legislator quasi infinita potentia instruatur legesque ad libitum creare, mutare, tollere valeat. Quanquam ab historicis hodie demonstratum est jus e moribus, id est e vita ipsa, parvis paulatim incrementis et sine legislatorum consiliis ortum esse, haec tamen opinio humanae menti tam penitus insidet ut in eadem multi etiam nunc perseverent. Qui autem illam accepit, omnem ordinem certum inesse societatibus humanis infitiari debet : leges enim ita, mores, instituta non e constanti quadam civitatis natura sed e fortuito casu penderent qui hunc aut illum legislatorem in ea suscitaverit. Si ex iisdem civibus, alio principe imperante, alia civitas exstare possit, eadem causa, iisdem circumstantiis, varios effectus gignendi facultatem habebit; rationali igitur vinculo res politicae carebunt.

Scientiae politicae nihil majorem moram attulit quam haec doctrina, in qua et philosophi vel prudentes vel inscii diutissime consenserunt. Nam cetera impedimenta, de quibus supra diximus aut infra loquemur, amoveri non poterant quamdiu hoc obstabat. Quamdiu in societatibus omnia adeo fortuita esse videbantur, nemini in mentem venire poterat per genera ac species

even though it comes from others. It is quite natural to think that things which are prior in knowledge are also prior in reality. And in political, legal and religious institutions, what is more visible and striking than the personalities of those who have ruled states, drawn up laws and given instruction on sacred rites? This is why the individual will of kings, legislators and prophets or priests comes across as the source of all political life. Their actions are performed in the sight of all and have nothing obscure about them. But the rest is difficult to see, lying hidden in the political system's secret functions. This is the origin of the very common myth that the legislator has almost infinite power, and can create, change or abolish laws at pleasure. Even though it has been shown by historians nowadays that law develops from *mores* – that is, from life itself – in a gradual step by step process unplanned by legislators, the idea has such a deep hold on the human mind that even now many persist in it. But its acceptance entails denial of any definite order in human societies. Laws, morals and institutions would depend, not on the fixed, stable nature of a state, but on whatever event had thrown up this or that particular legislator. If the same citizens, under a different ruler, can give rise to a different state, the same cause in the same circumstances would be able to bring about different effects. The realities of the political world would lack rational connexion.

Nothing has so obstructed the development of political science as this doctrine, that even philosophers, consciously or unconsciously, have so long accepted. Other obstacles, which we have already discussed or are going to discuss, could not be removed while it remained. It could not have occurred to anyone to divide human societies into classes and types as long as everything in them seemed so

eas dividere. Nulla enim genera in rebus existere possunt nisi sint causae quae in variis locis ac temporibus vim suam exhibeant eademque semper et ubique gignant. Praeterea si legislator vitam civilem arbitrio suo instituat et regat, ubi materiam aliquam scientiae invenies ? Omnis enim scientiae materia in rebus consistit quae natura sua stant et humanae voluntati reniti valent ; si contra in infinitum quasi tractabiles sint, nihil nos stimulabit ut eas observemus. Immo, iisdem nihil inerit quod observatio assequatur ; nam si quid proprium per se habeant, nemo eas ad libitum componere poterit. Inde fit ut Politica diu ars tantum fuerit.

At enim nemo unquam negavit humanae naturae scientiam necessariam esse, si quis homines regere velit. Concedo ; sed, ut supra monstravimus, haec scientia psychologia, non politica appellanda est ; nam ad hominem privatum, non ad civitatem pertinet. Ut vere politica scientia existat, oportet ut civitates naturam quamdam habeant quae ex ipsa partium natura e quibus constant earumque dispositione efficiatur et civilia facta gignat : quibus autem positis, fabulosa illa legislatoris persona evanescit.

IV

Attamen non satis est materiam aliquam habere scientiae idoneam. Si genera et leges in rebus imis ita absconduntur ut nullo pacto inde expediri possint, earum scientia in aeternum possibilis tantum manebit. Ut revera instituatur, necesse est aliquam methodum in promptu nobis esse, ad rerum naturam et ad scientiae requisita accommodatam.

Ne credas autem hanc sponte animis occurrere ubi

fortuitous. Types cannot exist unless there are causes which, at work in different times and places, always and everywhere produce the same effects. Besides, if the legislator establishes and directs social life as he wishes, where are we to find the material for a science? The subject matter of science consists only of things that have their own stable nature and a power to resist human will. If they were completely pliant, there would not be anything motivating us to observe them. Indeed, there would be nothing in them to get hold of through observation. If, however, they had their own inherent nature, no one could shape them at will. All of this is why for a long time Politics was only an art.

It is true that nobody interested in governing people has ever denied the need for a science of human nature. But, as we have already shown, this science should be called psychology, not politics. It concerns the individual, not the state. Political science truly exists only on the assumption that societies have a certain nature which results from the nature itself of the parts composing them and from their organization, and which generates social facts. Given this, the mythical figure of the legislator disappears.

IV

But it is not enough that science has a suitable subject matter. If laws and types are so concealed in the depths of things that there is no way of drawing them out, a science of them would forever remain a mere possibility. To establish it in fact, a method must be available to us, adapted to the nature of things and to the requirements of science.

This should not be thought to come spontaneously to

aditur scientia ; contra, non nisi multa tentando invenitur. Vide quam recenter animalium scientia viam repererit vitae leges in vivis ipsis observandi. Psychologia quoque diu erravit priusquam methodum propriam sibi composuerit ; politica autem scientia in majoribus etiam difficultatibus impeditur. Res enim tam variae sunt ut quod commune habent quasi velatum lateat; tam mobiles ut observatorem fugere videantur. Praeterea, causae et effectus ita inter se implicantur ut omni modo providendum sit ne aliae cum aliis confundantur. Ante omnia, nulla experimenta in societatibus humanis tentari possunt nec facile reperire est qua alia ratione pro experimento uti possimus. Vides methodum, antequam scientiam inchoaverimus, non constitui posse: e scientia oritur, quamvis eidem necessaria sit.

Quaeramus nunc quatenus varias illas conditiones, omni scientiae necessarias, in suo libro Secundatus expleverit.

mind with the beginning of a science. On the contrary, it takes much searching around to discover it. Consider how recently the science of animals has discovered a way of observing the laws of life in living beings themselves. Psychology, too, stumbled along for some time before it settled on its own method. Political science faces even greater difficulties. Things are so diverse that what they have in common lies, as if veiled, out of sight, so quick to change that they seem to run away from the observer. And causes and effects are so interwoven that every care must be taken not to confuse them with one another. Above all, it is impossible to make experiments with human societies and it is not easy to find another method to use instead. The method cannot be formed before we begin to develop the science. It arises out of the science, although it is necessary for it.

Let us now enquire to what extent these different conditions, necessary to all science, were met by Montesquieu in his book.

CAPUT SECUNDUM

QUATENUS SCIENTIAE POLITICAE MATERIAM PROPRIAM SECUNDATUS ASSIGNAVERIT

I

Mirum est toties disputatum esse quid Secundatus in libro suo sibi destinaverit : nempe in pluribus locis ipse nos monet quid propositum habeat. « Hoc opus, inquit, pro materia habet leges, mores variasque consuetudines omnium terrae populorum. Immensam hanc materiem merito appelles, quippe quae omnia instituta amplectatur quae apud homines valent. » [1] [a] Secundatus ergo res politicas ita tractare aggreditur ut eas, quales sint, scrutetur, « earum origines inquirat causasque reperiat, et quae in corporum et quae in animorum natura jacent. » [2] Legislatoris autem partes vires suas excedere humiliter declarat nedum eas affectet, neque praesertim eorum exemplum imitatur qui societatem ex integro reficere suscipiunt. « Non scribo, inquit, ut reprehendam quae in qualibet gente instituta sunt. Sed populus quisque in meo libro inveniet praeceptorum explicationem quae sequitur... Si res mihi ita succedere possit ut omnes cives novas rationes habeant, ut officia sua, suos principes, suam patriam, suas leges melius diligant et magis conscii suae felicitatis efficiantur, in

---

1. *Défense de l'Esprit des Lois ;* secunda pars, initio.
2. *Loc. cit.*

CHAPTER TWO

THE EXTENT TO WHICH MONTESQUIEU ASSIGNED POLITICAL SCIENCE ITS OWN SUBJECT MATTER

I

It is surprising that there has been so much argument over what it was that Montesquieu set out to do in his book. He states his aim in many places. "This work deals with the laws, customs and different practices of all the peoples of the earth. It may be said that its subject is vast, since it covers all the institutions in force amongst human beings."[1] [a] The objective which Montesquieu sets himself is a study of political realities in which he may investigate their nature, "seek their origins and find their causes, both in the physical domain and in that of the mind".[2] The role of the legislator, he says modestly, exceeds his powers, still less does he aspire to it, and in particular he does not imitate the example of those ready to rebuild society on a completely new basis. "I do not write to condemn what is established amongst any people whatsoever. Each nation will find in my book the explanation of the maxims it follows... If I could bring it about that everyone had new reasons for loving their duties, their rulers, their country and laws, and that they were made more aware of their good fortune in

---

1. *Defence of the Spirit of the Laws*, pt. 2, beginning.
2. *Loc. cit.*

quacumque regione aut civitate vivant, me omnium mortalium felicissimum esse censeam. » [1] [a]

Hoc consilium tanta cura exsecutus est ut multi eum etiam vituperaverint propterea quod nihil usquam vituperat, sed res ita reveretur ut ne judicare quidem eas audeat. Sane procul abest quin tam aequis oculis res humanas intueatur, eosque, qui hanc incuriam ei objecerunt, sensus operis sine dubio latet. [c] Multa tamen, quae a moribus nostris abhorrent et ab omnibus Europe populis hodie respuuntur, in quorumdam populorum natura bene fundata existimat. Sic quamdam servitutem, temperatam sane et humanam,[2] et jus plures uxores habendi[3] et falsas religiones[4] multaque alia ejusmodi quibusdam temporibus et locis apta esse censet ; immo hanc civitatis formam quam maxime odit, Tyrannida scilicet, Orientis gentibus necessariam arbitratur.

Ne autem inde concludas Secundatum omni quaestione quae ad usum pertinet abstinuisse. Ipse contra profitetur se inquirere « quae societati humanae summatim et singulis societatibus melius conveniant ;... quae per se aliquam utilitatem habeant, et, si duae consuetudines damnosae sint, quae majus, quae minus damnum secum afferat. » [5] Itaque, non tantum leges, sed vitae praecepta in ejus libro invenies ; non scientiam modo, sed artem. Immo vero non sine quadam ratione vituperari potest quod ea non satis separaverit. Non in una operis parte quod est, in altera quod esse debet quaeritur, sed ars et scientia ita inter se implicantur ut saepius ab una ad alteram sensim traducatur. Duas illas problematum series nondum distincte secernit,

---

1. *Praefatio*, cf. L. IV, C. 2, [b] nota : « On dit ici ce qui est et non pas ce qui doit être. »
2. XV, 6. [d]
3. XVI, 1 et passim.
4. XXIV, 25, 26. [e]
5. *Défense de l'Esprit des Lois* ; pars secunda.

whatever region or state they lived, I would think myself the happiest of mortals."[1] [a]

He carried out this project with such determination that many have criticized him because he never criticizes anything, but respects reality so much that he does not take it upon himself to judge it. Of course, it is far from the case that he surveys human affairs with this equanimity and detachment, and the sense of his work undoubtedly escapes those who accuse him of it. [c] Yet there are many things, incompatible with our own morality and nowadays rejected by all European peoples, which he thinks have a legitimate basis in the nature of others. He sees a form of slavery (albeit mild and humane),[2] polygamy,[3] false religions[4] and much else of the kind as appropriate in certain places and times. He even regards the type of government he most detests, despotism, as necessary amongst Oriental peoples.

But this does not mean that Montesquieu was un-concerned with practical problems. He himself makes clear that he wants to find out the things "which best suit human society and particular societies;...which are of benefit in themselves, and, if two practices are harmful, which involves greater harm, which less." [5] This is why we find in his book, not only laws, but maxims; not just science, but art. Indeed, he can be criticized, not without reason, for not separating these out enough. He does not go into what is the case in one part of his work, what ought to be in another, but art and science are so mixed together that there is often an almost imperceptible shift from one to the other. He does not yet make a clear distinction between the

---

1. Preface, cf. Bk. IV, ch. 2, [b] note: "This is to discuss what is and not what should be."
2. XV, 6. [d]
3. XVI, 1 and *passim*.
4. XXIV, 25, 26. [e]
5. *Defence of the Spirit of the Laws*, pt. 2.

sed simul agitat : quod non sine incommodo est, nam diversas methodos requirunt.

Ea autem confusio alia est quam quae apud priores philosophos in usu erat. Primum, scientia quae apud Secundatum invenitur vere politica est : nempe non de privati hominis conscientia tractat, sed res politicas pro materia habet. Nova illa igitur scientia, quamquam ab arte non satis discriminatur, certe existit. Praeterea, majorem libri partem occupat, nedum quaestionibus quae ad actum spectant obruatur. Arti praeest, nedum famuletur meliusque igitur suam naturam sequi potest. Scriptor enim sibi ante omnia proposuit quae sunt aut fuerunt cognoscere et explicare. Praecepta vero quae ediimtur nihil aliud plerumque sunt quam veritates, quas scientia methodo sua antea jam demonstraverit, in aliam quamdam linguam translatae. Non agitur enim nescio quam novam civitatem instaurare, sed justas civitatum formas definire : quod scientiae proprium est. Quia autem populo cuique salus suprema lex est,[1] ac societas servari nequit ni propriae suae naturae integritatem tueatur, satis est naturam illam describere ut quid petendum, quid fuguiendum sit, inde concludatur : morbus enim omni modo vitandus, quidquid contra salubre est optandum. Postquam, exempli gratia, Democratiam demonstravit in parvis civitatibus solum existere posse, praecipere [a] facile erat a nimia finium prolatione omni Democratiae abstinendum. In raris tantum casibus, ut melius infra videbimus,[2] evenit ut ars in scientiae locum sine jure succedat.

Ceterum ea ipsa praecepta, propterea quod nova via comparantur, longe differunt ab iis quae apud superiores scriptores politicos inveniuntur. Isti enim ideam quamdam, omnibus locis temporibusque supereminentem,

---

1. XXVI, 23.
2. V. infra, p.56 et sq.

two sets of problems, but tackles them all at once, and the trouble with this is that they demand different approaches.

But there is not the same confusion as amongst earlier philosophers. In the first place, Montesquieu's science genuinely is political science. It is not about the state of mind of the individual; its study is of political things. This new science, though not separated out enough from art, at least exists. Indeed, it occupies most of the book, far from being engulfed by an interest in practical questions. It takes precedence over art, far from being subordinated to it, and so can be more faithful to its own nature. The author's aim is above all to learn about and explain present or past realities. In most cases the maxims enunciated by him are only truths already established by science in its own way, but put in another language. His concern is not with instituting, somehow or other, a new state, but with identifying regular, well grounded forms of state, and this is a matter of science. Since, for every people, wellbeing is the supreme law,[1] and a society, to maintain itself, must guard the integrity of its own nature, it is enough to describe this nature to be in a position to work out from it what should be aimed at or avoided, for disease is in every way something to try to avoid and whatever is sound and healthy is desirable. For example, once he had shown that democracy can exist only in small states, it was easy to lay down that no democracy should attempt to extend its frontiers very far. It is only in a few cases – as we shall see more clearly later on[2] – that there is an unjustifiable move from science to art.

Moreover, because of the new way of establishing these precepts there is a great difference between them and those found amongst earlier writers on politics, the type who offered us some ideal, transcending time and place, that

---

1. XXVI, 23.
2. See below, pp. 56 *et sq.*

nobis offerebant quae toti humano generi convenire deberet. Unam civitatis formam, unam morum jurisque disciplinam esse confidebant quae omnium hominum naturae congrueret ; ceteras autem, quae in historia occurrunt, pravas aut saltem imperfectas esse et populorum imperitia tantum exstitisse. Nil vero mirum. Nam, cum ab historia oculos averterent, non sentire poterant hominem non semper et ubique eumdem esse, sed contra mobilem et varium, eamque igitur morum, legum, institutorum diversitatem in rerum natura fundatam. Contra Secundatus vitae regulas cum vitae conditionibus mutabiles esse intelligit. Cum in suis investigationibus diversae societatum species ei obversarentur quae aeque justae essent, ne venire quidem in mentem ei poterat praecepta, quae omnibus populis valerent, edicere ; sed eadem propriae cujusque generis naturae accommodat. Quod monarchiae appetendum est, idem democratiae fugiendum ; neque tamen monarchia, aut contra democratia, per se tantam excellentiam habet ut omnibus civitatibus anteponenda sit.[1] Sed, ex temporis locique conditionibus, modo haec, modo illa reipublicae forma convenit.[2] Secundatus ergo non adeo incuriosus est de rerum quas describit utilitate ; eas autem quaestiones alia ratione quam quae erat in usu tractat. Non omnia quae facta sunt laudat, sed quid bonum sit, quid non, e normis decernit quas e rebus ipsis traxit quaeque, ob eam causam, rerum varietati respondent.

---

1. « Il vaut mieux dire que le gouvernement le plus conforme à la nature est celui dont la disposition particulière se rapporte mieux à la disposition du peuple pour lequel il est établi. » (I, 3).

2. Miratur sane Monarchiam propterea quod in ejus compositione multo majorem artem invenit ; at non ideo existimat eam per se optimam reipublicae formam esse : contra, si forte in civitate quae paucos cives numerat instituatur, perituram societatem.

ought to apply to the whole of mankind. They were convinced that a single form of state and a single legal and moral doctrine fitted in with all men's nature, and that everything else, with an actual, historical existence, was perverse or at least imperfect, and came about only through people's inexperience. There is nothing surprising about this. Since they disregarded history they could not see that man is not always and everywhere the same, but varied and changeable, and that the diversity of morals, laws and institutions is therefore based on the nature of things. In contrast, Montesquieu understands that rules of life differ according to conditions of life. Since he was struck in his investigations by different, equally normal and well grounded types of society, it could not even cross his mind to lay down rules valid for all peoples. He adapts them to each type's own nature. Things are desirable in a monarchy that should be avoided in a democracy, and neither monarchy nor democracy has such great value in itself to make it preferable to all other political systems.[1] But, according to the conditions of time and place, sometimes this and sometimes that form of state is appropriate.[2] Montesquieu is not, then, so unconcerned with the practical value of the things he describes. However, his way of tackling these questions is different from what had been usual. He does not endorse every actuality, but decides what is or is not the good in terms of norms which he derived from things themselves and which accordingly correspond with the diversity of things.

---

1. "It is better to say that the government most in conformity with nature is the one with the particular organization that relates best to the character of the people for whom it is established." (I, 3).

2. No doubt he admires monarchy because he finds much greater art in its organization. But he does not on that account consider it the best form of commonwealth. On the contrary, if it happened to become established in a state with only a few citizens, the society would collapse.

II

Non modo Secundatus res civiles tanquam materiam observatori propositam attingit, sed easdem arbitratur distinctas ab iis quas ceterae scientiae tractant.

Leges quidem enumerat quae ex humana conditione, remota omni societate, sequantur quaeque igitur ad meram psychologiam pertineant ; eas naturae leges appellat.[1] Sed quales sint attende : jus vitam servandi aut in pace vivendi,[2] jus vescendi, jus utriusque sexus ad alterum inclinationi indulgendi,[3] denique jus commercia cum proximis habendi.[4] Addit quidem aliquem Dei sensum naturae legem primam esse secundum dignitatem, si non secundum tempora ; at non apertum est quem locum inter ceteras ea obtineat.[5] Quidquid id est, haec omnia, quemadmodum ex privata vita oriuntur, ita ad privatam vitam spectant, minime autem ad politicam, aut certe eam vix praeparant ; hic enim instinctus quo ad hominum commercium impelimur, si societati vias aperit, ejus formas, naturam, leges non efficit. Nihil est in civilibus institutis quod ea ratione explicari possit. Ceterum de tota quaestione

---

1. « Avant toutes ces lois, sont celles de la nature, ainsi nommées, parce qu'elles dérivent uniquement de la constitution de notre être. Pour les connaître bien, il faut considérer un homme avant l'établissement des sociétés. » (I, 2).

2. « L'homme, dans l'état de nature [...] songerait à la conservation de son être, avant de chercher l'origine de son être... On ne chercherait donc point à s'attaquer, et la paix serait la première loi naturelle. » (*Ibid.*, cf. XXVI, 3 et 7).

3. « La prière naturelle qu'ils se font toujours l'un (un sexe) à l'autre, serait une troisième loi. »

4. « Le désir de vivre en société est une quatrième loi naturelle. »

5. *Ibid.*, cf. *Défense*, etc., primae partis objectionem sextam. In aliis locis in jure naturali comprehendit quasdam domesticae vitae regulas (XXVI, 3 - 5, [a] 14) et pudoris leges (XV, 12, et XXVI, 3). Sed eas forsan ex utriusque sexus ad alterum appetitu sequi existimat.

II

Montesquieu not only treats social things as open to observation but considers them distinct from the subject matter of other sciences.

It is true that he draws up a list of laws which follow from the human condition, abstracted from all society, and which are therefore a matter of pure psychology. He calls them laws of nature.[1] But let us notice what they are: the right to protect one's life or to live in peace,[2] the right to eat, the right of each sex to gratify its desire for the other,[3] and the right of association with those close to us.[4] He adds that some sense of God is a first law of nature, in order of importance, if not chronologically. Yet its relation to the others is unclear.[5] In any case, just as all of them have their source in individual life so their concern is with individual life, not with the political, or at least they lay little basis for it. The impulse towards relationships with our fellow men, even if it opens the way to society, does not produce its forms, nature or laws. There is nothing about social institutions which can be explained by this approach. And Montesquieu is brief and

---

1. "Prior to all these laws are the laws of nature, so named because they derive uniquely from the constitution of our being. To understand them, it is necessary to consider a man prior to the establishment of societies." (I, 2).

2. "Man, in the state of nature [...], would think of the preservation of his being before looking for the origin of his being... Therefore there would not be any attempt to attack one another, and peace would be the first natural law." (*Ibid.*, cf. XXVI, 3 and 7).

3. "The natural suit that each (sex) always pays to the other would be a third law."

4. "The desire to live in society is a fourth natural law."

5. *Ibid.*, cf. *Defence of the Spirit of the Laws*, pt. 1, sixth objection. Elsewhere, he includes in natural law certain rules of domestic life (XXVI, 3 - 5, [a] 14) and laws of modesty (XV, 12 and XXVI, 3). But perhaps he thinks that they arise from each sex's desire for the other.

breviter ac strictim noster loquitur, quippe quae ad propositum suum non recte attineat ; sed eam tantum attingit ut materiam suam melius definiat, id est a rebus proximis discriminet.

Leges autem quae civitatem respiciunt a prioribus prorsus separat proprioque nomine appellat,[1] quia ex hominis natura deduci nequeunt. Eae sunt de quibus in ejus libro agitur ; ea est vera investigationis quam suscepit materia, scilicet jus gentium, jus civile, jus politicum, omnia denique praecipua societatis humanae instituta. Verba autem attente interpretemur. Quanquam varias illas juris formas naturales non vocat, attamen non eas existimat extra naturam esse, sed in rebus fundatas aliter atque priores ; nempe e natura non hominis, sed civitatum sequi. Earum causae, non in humana mente, sed in communis vitae conditionibus quaerendae sunt. Si, exempli gratia, juris civilis regulas apud quemdam populum intelligere velis, quomodo cives inter se consocientur, quis sit eorum numerus considerare debes ; si juris politici praecepta, quae sit principum privatorumque mutua conditio, etc. Sane, cum societates ex hominibus individuis tantummodo constent, earum natura a natura hominum pro parte pendet ; sed homo ipse alius est in diversis societatibus. Non eodem animi habitu est, non eadem cupit in Monarchia atque in Democratia aut in Tyrannide. Quod vero solas leges quae segregem vitam respiciunt naturales appellavit, quasi aliae illud nomen non mererentur, hoc temporis moribus imputandum est. Nam philosophi naturalem vocare solebant hominis statum qui sine societate viveret, ac naturale jus leges quae in tali statu observarentur. Secundatus verbum

---

1. *Lois positives* (I, 3).

sketchy in what he says on the whole question, which, indeed, is not of direct concern to his project. He touches on it only to have a better definition of his own subject matter, that is, to separate it out from related things.

He clearly distinguishes laws to do with the state from these others and gives them their own name,[1] because they cannot be deduced from human nature. They are what his book is about, the true subject matter of the investigation undertaken by him – international law, civil law, political law and all the great institutions of human society. Moreover, the terms he uses should be interpreted with care. Although he does not call these various forms of law natural, he does not regard them, even so, as outside nature, but as founded in things in a different way from the others, as following from the nature, not of man, but of political societies. Their causes are to be sought, not in the human mind, but in the conditions of collective life. If, say, our concern is with understanding the rules of civil law in a particular society, it is how people group themselves and how many of them there are that we need to consider; if it is with the maxims of political law, it is the relative position of ordinary citizens and their rulers, etc. Of course, since societies consist only of individual human beings, their nature depends in part on the nature of men. But man himself is different in different societies. He does not have the same way of thinking or the same desires in monarchy and democracy or in despotism. Montesquieu's talk of only laws of individual life as natural, as if the others did not merit the name, should be put down to usage at the time. Philosophers conventionally referred to a state in which man did not live in society as natural, and to laws in observance in this state as natural law. Montesquieu

---

1. "Positive laws" (I, 3).

cum usitato sensu retinuit, quamvis aliquid ambiguitatis haberet.

Hac doctrina novam juris philosophiam instauravit. Etenim, usque ad hoc tempus, philosophi de iis quaestionibus in duas partes scindebantur. Alii jus totum, non rerum natura fundatum, sed hominum libera voluntate et nescio qua originali stipulatione institutum esse docebant. Alii quamdam ejusdem partem — sed hanc tantum — naturalem esse arbitrabantur, scilicet eam quae ex universali hominis notione deduci poterat. Sola enim hominis privati natura ita definita et stabilis esse videbatur ut firmum juri fundamentum esse posset. A prioribus igitur philosophis non adeo isti dissentiebant ; nam, cum summa tantum et perpauca principia ad eam originem reduci queant, leges particulares, quae populorum codices implent, humana manu factas et ipsi habebant. Sane Hobbaeo aliisque, qui hominem ad vitam communem impetu naturali impulsum esse negabant, adversabantur, sed, si non societatem ipsam, certe civitatum formas et pleraque civilia instituta e mera conventione pendere arbitrabantur. Secundatus contra non modo generales illas regulas, sed totum legum contextum, quales apud diversas gentes vigent aut viguerent, naturalem esse profitetur ; eas autem ex natura corporis politici, non hominis derivat. Mire enim sensit naturam societatum non minus solidam atque immotam esse quam hominis, neque populos facilius quam animalia ex una specie ad aliam traduci posse. Nihil igitur iniquius sit quam si Secundatum cum Machiavelo compares, quippe qui leges tanquam machinas consideraverit quibus principes ad libitum uti possint. [a] Noster contra non minus stabile fundamentum juri subjecit quam Grotius ejusque sectatores, sed nova illa, quam diximus, ratione.

carried on with the term in its standard sense, despite the ambiguity involved.

His approach gave rise to a new philosophy of law. The issues, until then, split philosophers into two factions. Members of one taught that law in its entirety lacked foundation in the nature of things, but was established by human freewill and some sort of original contract. Members of the other considered that a part of law – but no more than this – was natural, namely that which could be deduced from a universal conception of man. It was only the nature of individual man which seemed settled and distinct enough to be a firm foundation of law. Therefore they did not differ that much from the other philosophers. Since only a very few, very general principles could be traced back to this origin, they themselves also regarded particular laws – and the legal codes of peoples are full of these – as a product of human artifice. Of course, they opposed Hobbes and others who denied that man was impelled by a natural urge towards collective life. But they believed in the dependence, if not of society itself, certainly of forms of state and of most social institutions on pure convention. In contrast, it is the whole fabric of laws in force in the past or present amongst different peoples, and not just some general rules, that Montesquieu recognizes as natural. But he derives them from the nature of the political system, not of man. He is remarkable for his understanding that the nature of societies is not less fixed and stable than the nature of man, and that it is no easier to change the species of a people than of a living being. It would be perverse to compare Montesquieu with Machiavelli, who considered laws mere instruments rulers could put to any use they wished. [a] Montesquieu placed law on as firm a foundation as Grotius and his followers, but in the new way we have discussed.

At enim, in pluribus operis sui loci, de quibusdam
principiis etiam civilis politicique juris ita loqui videtur
quasi per se stent neque a societatum natura pendeant.
« Antequam, inquit, leges institutae essent, quaedam
aequitatis relationes erant possibiles. Contendere nihil
justum, nihil injustum esse praeter id quod leges ab
hominibus institutae jubent aut vetant, idem est atque
negare circulorum radios inter se aequos fuisse antequam
ab aliqua manu descripti sint. » [1] [a]

Hoc autem iis quae supra exposuimus minime contra-
dicit. Nam propterea quod jus societatum natura fundatur,
non ideo asseritur nullum similitudinem inter populorum leges et mores existere. Sed, quemadmodum omnes
vel diversissimae civitates aliquid commune habent, ita
sunt quaedam leges quae in omni civitate occurrunt.
Eae sunt quas Secundatus societati humanae summatim
convenire dicit ; quae cum, ubicumque societas existit,
obversentur, in ipsa societatis notione implicantur
eaque expediri possunt. Itaque, ut earum veritas
bene demonstretur, non refert utrum ab hominibus
revera institutae sint an non, utrum societates existant,
an nunquam fuerint ; satis est si modo tanquam possibiles concipiantur.[2] Has leges in alio loco Secundatus
legem pure et universe appellat eamque nihil aliud esse
dicit quam rationem humanam, quatenus totius terrae
populos regat ;[3] nempe e societatis definitione, si semel
eam obtinuerimus, sola vi rationis deduci possunt. Eas
ceterum, quia apud omnes gentes occurrunt et quodam
sensu ante societatum institutionem esse concipiuntur,
a naturae legibus non distincte forsitan separavit.

---

1. I, 1.
2. « Il faut donc avouer des rapports d'équité antérieurs à la loi
positive qui les établit : comme, par exemple, que *supposé qu'il y eût des
sociétés des hommes,* [b] il serait juste de se conformer à leurs lois. » (*Ibid.*)
   3. I, 3. [c]

It may be objected that there are many passages in his work where he seems to talk of certain principles, even of civil and political law, as if they stand by themselves, independently of the nature of societies. He writes: "Before there existed established laws, there existed possible relations of equity. To maintain that nothing is just or unjust except that which humanly established laws order or prohibit is the same as to deny that the radii of circles were equal before anyone had drawn them." [1] [a]

Yet this does not at all contradict the views we have already set out and examined. It is not claimed that, because law is based on the nature of societies, there does not exist any similarity in the laws and morals of peoples. Instead, just as all, even very different, states have something in common, so there are certain laws that occur in every state. They are laws which Montesquieu says fit in with human society generally, and which, since observed wherever society exists, are implied in the very idea of society and can be explained by it. So it does not matter for the demonstration of their truth if men have in fact instituted them or not, and if there are or have never been societies. It is enough if they are simply conceivable as possible. [2] Elsewhere, Montesquieu calls these laws pure, universal *law*, and says it is none other than human reason in so far as it governs the peoples of all the earth[3] – for they can be deduced by the sole force of reason from the definition of society, if we ever laid hold of it. And perhaps he does not distinguish them clearly from laws of nature because they occur amongst all peoples and are conceived as prior, in some sense, to the institution of societies.

---

1. I, 1.
2. "It is therefore necessary to acknowledge relations of equity prior to the positive law that establishes them; for example, *given that there were societies of men,* [b] it would be right to conform to their laws ."(*Ibid.*)
    3. I, 3. [c]

Unum est quod ei doctrinae merito objici possit. Jus enim moralemque vitam, quae una est, in duas partes scindit quae neque eamdem originem neque eamdem naturam habeant. Non facile igitur videre est quomodo in unum coeant, praesertim quod saepe inter se discordes sunt. Nonnumquam enim evenit ut jus naturale et jus civile aut politicum contraria a nobis requirant ; cum nullum commune fundamentum habeant, unde decernetur cui sit obtemperandum ? Secundatus quidem existimare videtur naturae leges ante ceteras exsequendas esse.[1] Cur autem in omni casu hominis natura magis sacra sit quam societatis, eam noster quaestionem praeterit. Prioribus philosophis ea difficultas non existebat, quippe qui jus ex unico principio deducerent. Si vero duo principia sunt, nostra vita in duos sensus, inter se saepe contrarios, distrahitur. Una igitur via superest qua ex his angustiis evadere possimus, scilicet si ponitur omnes juris et morum regulas, etiam quae privatam vitam respiciunt, e societatis natura sequi. Secundatus autem in eo puncto velut in pluribus aliis, quamvis novam doctrinam instauret, priori tamen pro parte impeditus haeret.

---

1. V. XXVI, 3, 4, ac praesertim 5.

There is a single, well founded objection that can be made against this approach. It divides law and moral life, which are one, into two parts that do not have the same origin or the same nature. So it is not easy to see how they come together to form a whole, especially in view of frequent differences between them. It sometimes happens that natural law and civil or political law make conflicting demands on us. Where are we to go to decide which to comply with, given that they have no common basis? Montesquieu seems to believe that laws of nature should be accepted and followed before the others.[1] But why is man's nature always more sacred than society's? He passes over the question. The difficulty did not exist for earlier philosophers, who, of course, deduced law from a single principle. If in fact there are two principles, our life would be pulled in two, often completely opposite, directions. So only one way is left, by which we can escape these problems, namely if it is established that all legal and moral rules, even those concerning individual life, follow from the nature of society. But on this point as on many others, and even in initiating a new approach, Montesquieu is still attached to an older one and held back by it.

---

1. See XXVI, 3, 4 and especially 5.

CAPUT TERTIUM

QUOMODO CIVITATES PER GENERA AC SPECIES SECUNDATUS DIVISERIT

I

Secundatus quidem non societates, sed modos quibus gubernantur distinxisse atque igitur usitatam divisionem, aliquatenus mutatam, tantummodo videtur retulisse. Tria enim genera separat : Rempublicam, quae Aristocratiam Democratiamque comprehendit, Monarchiam et Tyrannida. Itaque Comte eum vehementer reprehendit propterea quod, deserto proposito quod in exordio libri exposuerat, ad formam aristotelici operis redierit.[1] Si vero rem proprius inspicies, constabit has doctrinas fronte tantum similes esse.

Earum diversitas jam manifesta fiet, si modo animadvertes non e numero gubernatorum, ex Aristotelis methodo, hanc divisionem deductam esse. Etenim Democratia et Aristocratia tanquam duae varietates unius ejusdemque generis a Secundato considerantur, quanquam in una omnes, in altera pauci tantummodo cives ad gubernaculum accedunt. Contra Monarchia et Tyrannis, quamvis in utraque imperium penes unum sit, duas, non modo dissimiles, sed etiam inter se plane adversas species constituunt. Itaque multi hanc partitionem insimulaverunt quasi confusam et ambiguam ; et merito quidem, si vere Secundatus in societatibus nihil aliud quam civitatis regimen respexisset. Ejus

---

1. *Cours de philosophie positive*, IV, 181. [b]

CHAPTER THREE

MONTESQUIEU'S CLASSIFICATION OF STATES AND SOCIETIES[a]

I

Montesquieu seems to classify the ways societies are governed rather than societies themselves, and so just to reproduce, with a few changes, a traditional scheme. The three types he identifies are, after all, the republic – which includes aristocracy and democracy – monarchy and despotism. Thus Comte very much criticizes him on the grounds that the project set out at the beginning of the book was abandoned, in a return to the form of an Aristotelian work.[1] But on closer examination it is plain that the two approaches have only a superficial resemblance.

The difference between them soon becomes apparent just by noticing that the classification is not derived, as in Aristotle's method, from the number of rulers. Democracy and aristocracy are in Montesquieu's view merely two varieties of the same type, although in one all citizens share in government, in the other only a few. In contrast, monarchy and despotism constitute two types which are not just different but even completely opposed, although power belongs, in both, to a single person. This is why many have attacked the classification as ambiguous and confused – and with reason, if Montesquieu really did not have an interest in anything in societies except the government of a state. However,

---

1. *Course of Positive Philosophy*, IV, 181. [b]

autem ea de re doctrina multo latius patet. Nam haec tria civitatum genera non modo principum numero rerumque publicarum administratione differunt, sed tota natura.

Hoc jam planum erit ubi intellexerimus quomodo ea distinxerit. Etenim, dum Aristoteles ejusque imitatores divisionem suam ex abstracta civitatis notione sumpserunt, Secundatus contra e rebus ipsis. Tria illa genera non ex aliquo principio, *a priori* posito, deduxit, sed societatum comparatione formavit, quas historia aut peregrinatorum relationibus, aut etiam suis ipsis peregrinationibus cognoverat. Itaque verborum sensus lateat nisi primum quaeramus quae gentes ibi significentur.

Rempublicam autem appellat non omnem societatem quae a toto populo aut quadam populi parte administretur, sed Graecas Italicasque antiquitatis civitates, quibus addendae sunt inclytae illae Italiae urbes quae medio aevo floruerunt.[1] Priores vero principem locum tenent ; in toto libro, quotiescumque de Republica agitur, manifestum est Romam, Athenas, Spartam ante scriptoris oculos versari. Hoc est cur Democratiam et Aristocratiam sub eumdem titulum, Rempublicam scilicet, coegerit. Nam cum apud illas civitates una aut altera forma pariter occurrerit, aut etiam alia alii apud eumdem populum successerit, non omnino separari poterant. Barbarorum contra gentes, quanquam ab universis civibus saepissime gubernantur, non sub eodem nomine confundit, ut postea videbimus, nec dubium est quin Galliam nostram, si formam quam sibi ipsa hodie dederit cognovisset, non inter Respublicas adnumerasset.

---

1. V. X, 8, et V, 8. [a]

his approach goes much wider. His three types of state are different, not just in the number of rulers and the administration of public affairs, but in their whole nature.

This is clear as soon as we understand how he distinguised between them. Where Aristotle and his imitators took their classification from an abstract idea of the state, Montesquieu based his on things themselves. He did not derive the three types from some *a priori* principle, but formed them through a comparison of societies that he knew about from history, or from accounts of travellers, or even from his own travels. This is why, to see what his terms mean, we must first ask who the peoples are they refer to.

He gives the name, *republic*, not to every society with government by all or a part of the people, but to the Greek and Italian city-states of the ancient world – though also to the great cities which flourished in Italy during the middle ages.[1] The others, nonetheless, have pride of place, and throughout the book, in discussing the republic, he is clearly preoccupied with Rome, Athens and Sparta. This explains why he brought democracy and aristocracy under the same description, of a republic. Both forms were equally common in these states, or even followed each other in succession in the same society, and so they could not be kept completely separate. However, as we shall go on to see, he excludes "barbarian" nations, although government in them was very often by the whole body of the people, and it is without doubt the case that if he had known of France in its present-day form he would not have counted it a republic.

---

1. See X, 8 and V, 8. [a]

Quod ad Monarchiam attinet, hanc societatis structuram apud magnos praesentis Europae populos unice reperit.[1] Eam enim antiquis populis necessario ignotam esse demonstrat ac primum apparuisse cum Germani in imperium romanum irruerunt ejusque partes inter se diviserunt.[2] Sane non ignorat Graecos Latinosque sub regibus diu vixisse ; haec autem heroicae aetatis constitutio a vera Monarchiae natura longe diversa esse ei videtur.[3] Denique Tyrannida, si, quodam sensu, e qualibet civitatis forma per corruptionem oriri potest, tamen in solo Oriente naturaliter extitisse arbitratur. Hoc verbo Turcos Persas multasque alias Asiae gentes designat quibus septentrionalis Europae populi adsciscendi sunt. Quis autem dubitet antiquas civitates, Orientalia regna et hodiernas occidentalis Europae nationes tres societatum species esse, inter se plane distinctas ?

II

Vide ceterum quomodo eas descripserit. Non alias ab aliis tantummodo discriminat propterea quod non eadem ratione gubernantur, sed quia partium numero, dispositione et cohaerentia differunt.

Respublica enim in parvis tantum urbibus floruit neque se ultra angustos fines unquam extendere potuit; hic est civitatum apud antiquos modus. Tyrannis contra apud immensos populos occurrit qui vastos tractus occupant, ut asiaticae gentes. Monarchia denique mediocrem amplitudinem habet et, quemadmodum

---

1. XI, 8.
2. XI, 8, et *Lettres persanes*, 131. [a]
3. « Le plan de cette constitution est opposé à celui de nos monarchies d'aujourd'hui. » (XI, 11.) [b]

As for monarchy, he finds this structure of society only amongst the great nations of modern Europe.[1] He shows that it could not have been known to the peoples of the ancient world, but made its first appearance when the Germans invaded the Roman empire and divided it up amongst themselves.[2] He acknowledges, of course, the long period when the Greeks and Latins lived under the rule of kings. But this institution of a heroic age seems to him far removed from the real nature of monarchy.[3] Finally, there is despotism. Although something like this can develop, as a result of corruption, in any form of state, he thinks it has existed naturally only in the east. In discussing it, he has in mind the Turks, Persians and many other Asian peoples, including, too, those of northern Europe. Can there then be any doubt that the ancient city-states, eastern despotisms and the modern nations of western Europe are three, wholly distinct types of society?

II

Let us see how he characterized them. He separates them out from one another, not just because they are not governed in the same way, but because they are different in the number, organization and cohesion of their component parts.

The republic flourished only in small towns, and never managed to expand beyond narrow limits; this is the form of the ancient city-states. Despotism, in contrast, occurs amongst immense populations that occupy vast tracts of land, as with the nations of Asia. Monarchy, lastly, is moderate in size and in the same way that it

---

1. XI, 8.

2. XI, 8, and *Persian Letters*, 131. [a]

3. "The plan of this constitution is the opposite of that of our monarchies today." (XI, 11). [b]

civium numero Rempublicam superat, sic a Tyrannide superatur.[1]

Praeterea cives in diversis illis societatibus non eodem ordine disponuntur neque iisdem vinculis consociantur.

In Republica, ac praesertim in Democratia, omnes inter se pares sunt, immo similes. Civitas, ut ita dicam, molis speciem habet cujus partes ejusdem naturae sunt aliaeque juxta alias, nulla supereminente, collocantur. Omnes enim de re communi aeque curant ; qui magistratus habent, non ceteris superiores sunt, quia honores in tempus tantum gerunt. Quin, et in privata vita non multo magis inter se differunt. Etenim ne quis nimium opibus praestet, Reipublicae principium est,[2] aut saltem id ad quod tendit ; nam, si absoluta aequalitas non facile perfici potest, certe, ubicumque Respublica existit, leges obstant quin privatorum divitiae inter se nimis distent.[3] Hoc autem fieri nequeat si quisque in immensum fortunas suas augere possit ; sed necessarium est facultates omnium mediocres esse ut satis aequae sint. Frugalitas, ut ait noster, aequalitatis conditio est. « Cum singuli, inquit, eamdem felicitatem capessere debeant, iisdem voluptatibus frui eademque sperare debent ; quod non comparari potest nisi omnium frugalitate. » [4] [a]

His conditionibus, res privatae, cum adeo exiguae sint, non multum loci in cujusque vita et mente obtinent, quam contra totam implet communis utilitatis cura. Causa ergo deest ex qua diversitas inter homines praecipue oritur. Quin etiam, haec ipsa privata vita non adeo diversa esse potest. Nempe legitima illa universorum civium mediocritas omnes ferme ad commer-

---

1. V. VIII, 15-20.

2. V, 3 et sq.

3. V, 5.

4. V, 3. « Le bon sens et le bonheur des particuliers consiste beaucoup dans la médiocrité de leurs talents et de leurs fortunes. » (*Ibid.*)

exceeds, in the number of its subjects, the republic, it is exceeded in turn by despotism.[1]

Moreover, members of these different societies are not organized in the same structure or united by the same ties.

In a republic, and especially in a democracy, everyone is equal, indeed, alike. The state resembles a massive barrier wall in which the parts are of the same material and stand side by side, with none rising up above the others. Everyone is just as concerned for the common interest, and those in authority are not superior to the rest, since they hold office only for a time. Differences are not all that greater even in private life. It is a principle of the republic that nobody stands out very much in regard to wealth.[2] Or at least this is something it works towards. An absolute equality might be difficult to achieve, but wherever a republic exists the laws oppose huge disparities in individual wealth.[3] It could not come about at all, without limits to how far each can enrich themselves; everyone must have modest means, to be sufficiently equal. Frugalness, he says, is the condition of equality: "Since each should enjoy the same good fortune, they should taste the same pleasures and expect the same things – something that can come only from the general frugalness".[4] [a]

In these conditions private wealth has too small a place to be important in the individual's life and outlook; everyone is preoccupied, instead, with the common good. Hence the main source of difference among men does not exist – and there cannot be much difference in private life itself. The modest attitudes and circumstances, that the law lays down for everyone, destroy almost every incentive to

---

1. See VIII, 15-20.
2. V, 3 *et sq.*
3. V, 5.
4. V, 3. "The good sense and happiness of individuals largely consists in the mediocrity of their talents and fortunes." (*Ibid.*)

cium stimulos tollit, quippe quod sine quadam conditionum inaequalitate difficile existat.[1] Itaque singuli
fere eadem agunt ; scilicet, ex quadam terrae portione,
quae omnibus aequa est, quae ad vivendum necessaria
sunt quaerere laborant.[2] Uno verbo, omnis laboris
divisio deest inter corporis politici partes, nisi hoc
nomine appellare velimus hanc, de qua diximus,
alternis vicibus publicorum magistratuum functionem.
Ea quidem pictura Democratiae naturam potius exprimit ; Aristocratiam autem, cum Secundato adulterata
Democratia esse videatur (eam enim eo magis perfectam
esse censet quo Democratiae similior)[3] sine erroris
periculo omittere licet.

Quid autem, in tali societate, omnium civium voluntates conspirantes efficiat, facile intelligis. [b] Nempe patriae
imago animos tenet, dum singuli propriae suae utilitatis
incuriosi sunt, quia nihil fere proprium habent ; nihil
est igitur quod eos in contrarias partes distrahat. Ea est
virtus illa quae Secundato Reipublicae esse fundamentum videtur. Eo enim nomine non virtutem ethicam
appellat, sed politicam quae consistit in patriae amore
quaque nos nostraque civitati posthabemus.[4] Verbum
quidem merito reprehendi potest quod ambiguum est ;
attamen nil mirum si Secundato in mentem sponte
occurrerit. Nonne enim virtutem appellamus omnem
animi habitum qui nimiam privatae utilitatis curam
moderatur ? Hic autem in Republica necessario apud

---

1. V, 6, [a] et IV, 6.

2. « L'amour de la frugalité borne le désir d'avoir à l'attention que
demande le nécessaire pour sa famille. » (V, 3.)

3. « Plus une aristocratie approchera de la démocratie, plus elle sera
parfaite. » (II, 3.)

4. « On peut définir cette vertu, l'amour des lois et de la patrie. Cet
amour, demandant une préférence continuelle de l'intérêt public au sien
propre, donne toutes les vertus particulières : elle ne sont que cette
préférence. » (IV, 5.)

commerce, since it is difficult for this to exist without an inequality of conditions.[1] And so individuals do more or less the same thing. They work a piece of land, which is the same size for everyone, and try to meet their subsistence needs from it.[2] In sum, there is no division of labour amongst members of the political system – unless we want to apply the term to the rotation of public office, already discussed. It is a picture that expresses, above all, the nature of democracy. What about aristocracy? Since this seems, to Montesquieu, a corruption of democracy (he thinks it is more perfect, the more it is like democracy),[3] it may be disregarded without risk of misrepresentation.

It is easy to understand what it is, in such a society, that brings everyone together in a unity of will.[b] The idea of country is all-powerful, while individuals, having almost nothing of their own, are unmindful of their own interests. So there is nothing that draws them apart into opposing factions. This is the virtue that seems to Montesquieu the foundation of the republic. It is what he calls political – rather than moral – virtue, which lies in love of country, and in which we attach less importance to ourselves and our own concerns than to the state.[4] The term is open to criticism as ambiguous. However, it is not at all odd that Montesquieu hit on it. Do we not call virtue the whole nature and turn of character that limits preoccupation with self-interest? This must exist, in a republic, in everyone

---

1. V, 6 [a] and IV, 6.

2. "Love of frugalness limits the desire to possess to the concern required by family needs." (V, 3).

3. "The more an aristocracy approaches democracy, the more perfect it will be." (II, 3).

4. "This virtue can be defined as love of the laws and of country. This love, requiring a continual preference for the public interest over one's own, gives rise to all the individual virtues: they are just this preference." (IV, 5).

omnes existit, quoniam civitatis anima, si dicere liceat, cujusque menti insidet, ac contra, ex universa frugalitate, sui amor ipsa materia eget qua ali possit. Cum in cujusque conscientia ea pars, quae civitatem exprimit et in omnibus eadem est, ampla et valida sit, illa contra quae nos tantum nostrasque privatas res respicit exigua et imbellis, cives, non vi externa impulsi, sed impetu naturali, a se ipsis, ut ita dicam, ad commune bonum convertuntur.

Longe alia est Monarchiae natura. In ea omnia officia non modo publicae, sed etiam privatae vitae inter varias civium classes dividuntur. Alii agriculturam, alii commercium, alii artes colunt ;[1] sunt qui leges creant, qui contra eas exsequuntur sive judicando, sive gubernando,[2] ac nemini licet a parte sua discedere alienamque invadere.[3] [a] Itaque Monarchia principis unius imperio definiri non potest. Ceterum ipse Secundatus addit nullam societatem hoc nomine appellandam esse etiamsi ab uno regatur, ni leges sint fixae rataeque e quibus rex gubernet quasque arbitrio suo mutare non valeat.[4] Hoc autem continet certos ordines esse qui hujus potestatem moderentur. Quamvis supra eos stet, necessarium tamen est eosdem quadam vi propria praeditos esse neque adeo principi impares ut ei resistere nequeant. Finge enim huic auctoritati nihil obstare ; nulla lex esse potest quae principis voluntatem contineat, propterea quod leges ipsae ab unica ejus voluntate pendeant.

---

1. « Pour que l'état monarchique se soutienne, le luxe doit aller en croissant, du laboureur à l'artisan, au négociant, aux nobles, aux magistrats, etc. » (VII, 4.)

2. XI, 6.

3. « Toutes ces prérogatives seront particulières à la noblesse, et ne passeront point au peuple, si l'on ne veut choquer le principe du gouvernement. » (V, 9.) — « Il est contre l'esprit du commerce que la noblesse le fasse dans la monarchie. » (XX, 21. Cf. XI, 6.)

4. II, 1.

– each is imbued with what we might say is the collective spirit, and because of the general frugalness self-love lacks the very things letting it take root and thrive. The part of each person's consciousness which expresses society and which is the same in everyone is large and powerful, while the part to do only with ourselves and our own individual concerns is small and feeble. So it is not by an external force, but by a natural impulse, that people turn away from themselves, as it were, and towards the common good.

The nature of monarchy is quite unlike this. It involves a division amongst different social classes of all the functions of private as well as public life. Some engage in agriculture, some in commerce, some in industry and the arts,[1] while some make laws, others, in the judiciary or the administration, implement them,[2] and nobody is allowed to move away from their own role and into another.[3] [a] The definition of monarchy, then, cannot be that one person is sovereign. Montesquieu himself adds that no society should be described by this term, even if it is ruled over by a king, unless there are fixed and definite laws according to which he governs and which he cannot change just as he decides.[4] This involves the existence of established social orders that hold his power in check. Although he is placed above them, they need a power of their own and must not to be so unequal that they cannot resist him. If nothing stood in the way of the ruler's authority, there could not be any law that limits his will, since the laws themselves would depend solely on it.

---

1. "Thus, for the monarchical state to sustain itself, luxury must grow and increase, from the farmworker to the artisan, to the merchant, to the nobles, to the magistrates," etc. (VII, 4).

2. XI, 6.

3. "All these privileges will be peculiar to the nobility and will not transfer to the people, unless one wishes to upset the principle of the government." (V, 9) – "It is against the spirit of commerce for the nobility to engage in it in a monarchy." (XX, 21. *Cf.* XI, 6).

4. II, 1.

Hoc est quo Monarchia differt a ceteris civitatibus :
scilicet, laboris partitio, quae in Republica nulla erat,
hic maxima incrementa capessivit.[1] Societas igitur animali
bene comparari possit cujus partes, pro sua quaeque natura,
diversa agunt.

Hoc est cur Secundatus politicam libertatem Monarchiae
peculiarem existimet.[2] Etenim classes aut, si nostris
temporibus maxime usitato verbo uti liceat, politici corporis
organa non modo principem, sed se ipsa mutuo
moderantur. Nam, cum unumquodque eorum a ceteris
impediatur quin in infinitum crescat et totas corporis vires
ad se trahat, singula suam naturam sine obstaculis, at non
sine modo, explicare valent. Nunc intelligis quem locum
apud Secundatum obtineat inclyta illa de magistratuum
divisione doctrina ; nihil aliud est nisi forma singularis
hujus principii ex quo diversa publica munera inter diversas
manus dividi debent. Secundatus tantum momentum huic
partitioni attribuit, non ut omnem inter varios magistratus
discordiam tollat, sed contra ut melius inter se certent ne
quis eorum ceteros exsuperet et ad nihilum redigat.[3]

Sociale[a] igitur vinculum non idem esse potest atque
in Republica. Quaeque enim classis, cum exiguam
tantum politicae vitae partem amplectatur, nihil videt
ultra munus quod explet. Itaque non patriae, sed classis

---

1. « Les pouvoirs intermédiaires, subordonnés et dépendants,
constituent la nature du gouvernement monarchique. » (II, 4) — « Les
monarchies se corrompent lorsqu'on ôte peu à peu les prérogatives des
corps ou les privilèges des villes. » (VIII, 6) — « La monarchie se perd,
lorsqu'un prince... ôte les fonctions naturelles des uns pour les donner
arbitrairement à d'autres. » (*Ibid.*)

2. « La démocratie et l'aristocratie ne sont point des états libres par
leur nature. » (XI, 4)

3. « La liberté politique ne se trouve que dans les gouvernements
modérés. Mais elle n'est pas toujours dans les états modérés : elle n'y est
que lorsqu'un n'abuse pas du pouvoir... Pour qu'on ne puisse abuser du
pouvoir, il faut que, par la disposition des choses, le pouvoir arrête le
pouvoir. » (*Ibid.*)

The difference between monarchy and other states is that in it the division of labour, which does not exist in a republic, tends towards its fullest development.[1] Society might be compared with a living being, in which each part has a different function in line with its own nature.

This is why Montesquieu thinks that political freedom is specific to monarchy.[2] The classes or, in a widely used term nowadays, the *organs* of the political system act as a check, not just on the ruler, but on one another. Since each is prevented by the others from growing too powerful and absorbing all the energies of the whole, each can develop their own nature without hindrance, but not without limit. We can now understand the place, in Montesquieu's overall approach, of the famous theory of the division of powers. It is only a particular form of the principle that there should be a division of different functions of social, public life amongst different people. It has so much importance for him, not as a way of eliminating conflict between the various powers, but, on the contrary, to create a rivalry in which none can gain complete control and reduce the others to nothing.[3]

As a result, the social[a] bond cannot be the same as in a republic. Each class is involved in only a small part of political life and sees nothing beyond the horizons of its own activities and concerns. So it is the idea, not of

---

1. "Intermediate, subordinate and dependent powers constitute the nature of monarchical government." (II, 4) – "Monarchies are corrupted when there is a gradual removal of the prerogatives of the established social orders and of the privileges of the towns." (VIII, 6) – "Monarchy is destroyed when a prince... takes away the functions that are natural to some to give them arbitrarily to others." (*Ibid.*)

2. "Democracy and aristocracy are not free states by their nature." (XI, 4).

3. "Political liberty is found only in moderate governments. But it does not always exist in moderate states: it is present only when power is not abused... So that one cannot abuse power, power must check power by the arrangement of things." (*Ibid.*)

imago animos tenet : quisque ordo ad id solum tendit
ut ipse crescat, non ut res communis augeatur. Immo
et privatus quisque civis sibi ipse magis consulit. Etenim,
dum, in Republica, ex omnium aequalitate universa
frugalitas necessario sequitur, illa contra diversitas
cupiditates irritat. Sunt varii gradus honorum, dignitatum,
divitiarum, potestatis, ita ut quisque ante oculos habeat
aliquam vitae conditionem quae sua ipsius superior
est quamque ideo concupiscit.[1] Omnia igitur cives
a communi utilitate ad privatam convertunt ita ut
omnes virtutis illius, quae reipublicae fundamentum est,
desint conditiones.[2] Sed partium cohaerentia ex ipsa
earum diversitate oritur. Haec enim ambitio quae ordines
et privatos movet, eosdem stimulat ut munere quisque
suo quam optime fungatur. Itaque commune bonum
velut inscii assequuntur dum privata tantum commoda
affectare se credunt.[3] Hoc ipsum inter varias societatis
partes certamen earumdem conspirationem efficit.

Hoc stimulus vitae publicae in Monarchia a Secundato
honor appellatur.[4] Hoc verbo privatam seu civium seu
classium ambitionem designat ex qua nemo conditionem
suam deminui libenter patitur, sed contra eamdem quam
maxime extollere tentat.[5] Quod ceterum non fieri

---

1. « Le gouvernement monarchique suppose, comme nous avons dit,
[des prééminences,] des rangs, et même une noblesse d'origine. La nature
de l'*honneur* est de demander des préférences et des distinctions ; il est
donc, par la chose même, placé dans ce gouvernement. » (III, 7.)

2. « Les vertus qu'on nous y montre sont toujours moins ce que l'on
doit aux autres, que ce que l'on se doit à soi-même : elles ne sont pas tant
ce qui nous appelle vers nos concitoyens, que ce qui nous en distingue. »
(IV, 2 *initio.*)

3. « Il se trouve que chacun va au bien commun, croyant aller à ses
intérêts particuliers. » (III, 7.)

4. « L'honneur fait mouvoir toutes les parties du corps politique; *il les
lie par son action même.* [a] » (III, 7.)

5. « L'ambition est pernicieuse dans une république. Elle a de bons
effets dans la monarchie; elle donne la vie à ce gouvernement. » (*Ibid.*) —
« L'HONNEUR, c'est-à-dire le préjugé de chaque personne et de chaque
condition. » (III, 6. Cf.XX, 22.)

country, but class that is all-powerful. Each social order aims only at its own aggrandizement, not the advance of the common good. Indeed, each individual citizen is more concerned with their own interests. Where, in a republic, everyone's equality must lead to a general frugalness, here, in contrast, diversity stirs up avarice and ambition. There are different degrees of honour, rank, wealth and power, so that everyone is struck by another condition of life superior to their own and that they therefore want for themselves.[1] Everything thus has the effect of turning them away from common towards private interests, and all the conditions of the virtue which is the basis of a republic are absent.[2] Yet their diversity is in fact a source of cohesion. The ambition which motivates both individuals and groups drives them on so that they each perform their particular functions as well as possible. So, without knowing it, they bring about the public good, and believe all along that they act only for private gain.[3] It is the conflict between the different parts of society that produces their union.

Montesquieu talks of this stimulus to public life in monarchy as *honour*.[4] He uses the term to describe a private ambition, of individuals or social classes, in which far from accepting a fall in their own standing they try to increase this as much as they can.[5] It cannot come about

---

1. "Monarchical government presupposes, as we have said, [pre-eminences,] ranks, and even a hereditary nobility. The nature of *honour* is to demand preferences and distinctions, so that in and of itself it has a place in this government." (III, 7).

2. "The virtues we are shown here are always less what one owes others than what one owes oneself: they are not so much what draws us towards our fellow citizens as what distinguishes us from them." (IV, 2, beginning).

3. "It turns out that they each act for the common good, believing they act for their individual interests." (III, 7).

4. "Honour sets all the parts of the political system in motion; *its very action unites them.*[a]" (III, 7).

5. "Ambition is pernicious in a republic. It has good effects in monarchy; it gives life to this government." (*Ibid.*) – "HONOUR, that is, the prejudice of each person and each condition." (III, 6. *Cf.* XX, 22).

potest nisi hominibus satis alta indoles sit et quaedam libertatis dignitatisque cura quae non pulchritudine caret.[1] Attamen cum *honor* nimium sui amorem excitare possit, in vitium facile vertitur. Eam ob causam, Secundatus in pluribus locis non sine severitate de eo ideoque de Monarchiae moribus loquitur.[2] Ne credas autem nostrum hoc judicio Monarchiam elevare voluisse. Haec enim quae fatetur damna ex eo tantum oriuntur quod privatae res increverunt privatique majore libertate fruuntur ad suam utilitatem insequendam. Ceterum virtutem adeo arduam et raram esse existimat ut prudentis esse ei videatur illa quam parcissime uti. Itaque sapientissimam illam societatis compositionem, quae sine virtute homines cogit ut magna suscipiant, tantum miratur ut vitia quaedam facile ei condonet.[3]

De Tyrannide brevius loquar quam Secundatus ipse minore cura videtur descripsisse. Ceterum medium inter priores societates locum tenet. Tyrannis enim Monarchia quaedam est in qua omnes ordines aboleantur[4] ac sine ulla laboris divisione, aut Democratia in qua universi cives, excepto principe, inter se pares sint, sed in servitute.[5] Portentosi igitur animalis speciem

---

1. « (L'honneur) veut qu'on puisse indifféremment aspirer aux emplois, ou les refuser ; il tient cette liberté au-dessus de la fortune même. L'honneur a donc ses règles suprêmes [...]. Les principales[a] sont, qu'il nous est bien permis de faire cas de notre fortune, mais qu'il nous est souverainement défendu d'en faire aucun de notre vie. La seconde est que, lorsque nous avons été une fois placés dans un rang, nous ne devons rien faire ni souffrir qui fasse voir que nous nous tenons inférieurs à ce rang même. » (IV, 2.)

2. Vide locos apud Janet, *Hist. de la Science politique,* 3e édit., II, 469.[b]

3. « Dans les monarchies, la politique fait faire les grandes choses avec le moins de vertu qu'elle peut ; comme dans les plus belles machines, l'art emploie aussi peu de mouvements, de forces et de roues qu'il est possible. » (III, 5.)[c]

4. VIII, 6, initio.

5. « Les hommes sont tous égaux dans le gouvernement républicain; ils sont égaux dans le gouvernement despotique : dans le premier, c'est parce qu'ils sont tout ; dans le second, c'est parce qu'ils ne sont rien. » (VI, 2)

unless men have enough strength of character and a passion for freedom and dignity that does not lack splendour.[1] But honour easily becomes a fault, since it can be the source of an excessive self-love. This is why, in a number of passages, Montesquieu is quite severe about it, and so about morals, in general, in monarchy.[2] But it should not be thought that in making this criticism he intended to devalue monarchy. Although he brings out things that are wrong with it, they arise only because of the growth of a private sphere and the greater freedom of individuals to pursue their own interests and affairs. Moreover, he regards virtue as so unusual and difficult to attain that in his view it is sensible to rely on it as little as possible. The wisest organization of society is one that does without virtue in getting men to do great things, and he so admires this he readily overlooks faults in it.[3]

I shall be briefer about despotism, which Montesquieu himself seems to have portrayed with less care and attention. It occupies a middle position between the other societies. Despotism is a monarchy in which social orders have all been abolished[4] and there is no division of labour, or a democracy in which everyone, except the ruler, is equal, but in servitude.[5] It is like a monster in which only

---

1. "(Honour) expects that one can as happily aspire to office as turn it down; it sets this liberty above fortune itself. Honour therefore has its supreme rules... In the most important of all, we may well set store on our fortune but we are absolutely forbidden to set any on our life. The second is that, once placed in a particular rank, we should not do or allow anything that might show we consider ourselves inferior to the rank itself." (IV, 2).

2. See, for these passages, Janet, *History of Political Science*, 3rd ed., vol. II, 469. [b]

3. "In monarchies, politics brings about great things with as little virtue as it can, just as in the finest machines art employs as few motions, forces and wheels as possible." (III, 5). [c]

4. VIII, 6, beginning.

5. "Men are all equal in republican government; they are equal in despotic government; in the first, it is because they are everything; in the second, it is because they are nothing." (VI, 2).

offert in qua caput solum vivit, quippe quod totus corporis vires ad se traxerit.[1] Itaque neque virtus vitae publicae principium esse potest quia populus res communes ignorat, neque *honos* quia nulla diversitas existit. Homines societati vinciuntur propterea quod adeo imbelles sunt ut principis voluntatem non resistentes sequantur, id est solo metu.[2]

Hoc satis est ut plane demonstretur veras societatum species a Secundato distinctas esse. Id etiam manifestius fiat si in singula descendas. Nam non structurae modo principia diversa sunt, sed tota vita. Mores,[3] religiones,[4] familia,[5] matrimonium,[6] puerorum institutio,[7] crimina et poenae[8] non eadem sunt in Republica atque in Tyrannide aut in Monarchia. Immo societatum differentias animadvertisse potius videtur quam ea quae omnibus communia sunt.

III

At enim, si vere societatum species separaverit ac descripserit, cur eas ita definiit et his nominibus appellavit? Nempe non ex laboris divisione, non e socialis vinculi natura illas distinguit et nominat, sed ex unica summae auctoritatis constitutione.

Haec autem inter se non repugnant. Etenim necessarium erat unumquodque genus ea proprietate notare

---

1. « Le despotisme se suffit à lui-même ; tout est vide autour de lui. » (VI, 1, in fine.)
2. III, 9.
3. XIX. [a]
4. XXIV-XXV. [b]
5. XXIII, 2 et sq. [c]
6. XVI. [d]
7. IV.
8. XII, 18 et. sq. [e]

the head is alive, having absorbed all the energies of the body.[1] And so the principle of social life cannot be virtue, since the people do not have any knowledge of collective interests and affairs, and it cannot be *honour*, since there is not any diversity. Men are bound to society through their passiveness and unresisting obedience to the ruler's will, that is, only through fear.[2]

This is enough to make clear that the types of society distinguished by Montesquieu are real. It would become even more evident if we went into detail. They differ not only in basic structure but in their whole life. Morals,[3] religion,[4] family,[5] marriage,[6] education,[7] and crime and punishment[8] are not the same in a republic as in despotism or in monarchy. Indeed, he seems to have been more interested in differences between societies than in things that they all have in common.

III

Yet if it is in fact types of societies that were separated out and described by him, why is it he defined and named them in the way he did? Instead of going to the division of labour or the nature of the social bond, he distinguishes and names them just according to forms of sovereign power.

But these are not incompatible approaches. It was necessary to identify each type in terms of its most

---

1. "Despotism is self-sufficient: everything around it is empty" (VI, 1, conclusion).
2. III, 9.
3. XIX. [a]
4. XXIV-XXV. [b]
5. XXIII, 2 *et sq.* [c]
6. XVI. [d]
7. IV.
8 XII, 18 *et sq.* [e]

quae in eodem praecipua est et quam ceterae sequuntur. Primo autem adspectu, forma gubernationis hanc conditionem videtur explere. Nihil enim magis conspicuum est in publica vita ; nihil magis in se omnium oculos movet. Cum princeps in societatis, ut ita dicam, culmine stet et corporis politici caput saepe neque immerito appelletur, ab eo omnia pendere existimantur. Adde quod, cum philosophi ad hoc tempus nihil aliud in politicis rebus reperissent quod per genera et species dividi posset, difficile Secundato erat, quamvis novum aliquid ipse tentaret, eorum doctrinam omnino exuere. Ea causa est quare formas societatum e gubernationis formis discernere susceperit. Sane multa methodo objici possunt quam secutus est. Hoc enim signum nihil per se proprii ac peculiaris habet, sed, ut jam monstravimus, summi imperii natura mutari potest dum natura societatis immutata manet, aut contra una et eadem esse in societatibus quae longissime inter se distant. Sed error verbis potius quam rebus inest ; nam praeter quae ad populi regimen pertinent, multa alia enumerat quibus societates alias ab aliis discriminat.

Immo vero, si verba quibus utitur negligimus, nihil forsan in toto opere reperietur quod verius et acutius sit quam haec divisio cujus principia etiam nunc servari possunt. Etenim, non solum tres illae vitae communis formae quas descripsit tres distinctas species revera constituunt, sed etiam earum descriptio, qualem in ejus libro invenimus, earumdem naturam propriasque differentias non sine quadam veritate exprimit. Sane in antiquis civitatibus aequalitas et frugalitas non tantae fuerunt quantas Secundatus credidit. Attamen constat in iis, praesertim si cum hodiernis populis comparentur, privatas res angustissimum spatium habuisse quo se extenderent, communes contra amplum. Mire sensit

important property, from which the others derive. And at first sight it is the form of government which seems to meet this condition. Nothing is more striking in public life; nothing has greater hold of everyone's attention. Since the ruler stands, it might be said, at the "summit" of society and is often, quite understandably, called the "head" of the political system, everything is thought dependent on him. Nor, until Montesquieu's time, had philosophers come up with anything else in political life that could serve as a basis of classification. So it was difficult for him, even in attempting something new, to drop their approach altogether. This is why he tried to distinguish forms of society through forms of government – a method open, of course, to many objections. It uses a criterion with nothing fixed and specific about it. As already shown, the nature of sovereign power can change while the nature of society remains stable, or it can be one and the same in societies that are wholly different. But his mistake is at bottom a matter of terminology, not substance. In distinguishing societies from one another, he takes account of many other things besides those to do with a people's government.

In fact, if we set terminology aside, perhaps nothing in the whole work will be found more truthful and penetrating than this classification, the principles of which can stand even now. It is not just that he identified three forms of social life that constitute three distinct types in reality. It is also that the portrayal of them in his book is basically successful in capturing their nature and their essential, characteristic differences. Of course, equality and frugalness were not as great in ancient city-states as Montesquieu thought. Yet it is clear – especially if they are compared with modern society – that the area taken up in them by private interests and concerns was very small, while in the case of collective matters it was large. He had an admirable

Romae et Athenis pauca cujusque civis propria fuisse,
atque hanc fuisse causam qua societas fieret una. Contra,
apud nos, privatae vitae fines latius prolatae sunt ;
unusquisque nostrum suam indolem habet, suas opiniones, suos mores, suam religionem, seque et suas res a
societate publicisque rebus penitus secernit. Populi
igitur consensus non idem esse neque ex eadem origine
oriri potest, sed ex laboris divisione quae cives et ordines alios aliis necessarios efficit. Denique hoc genus,
quod Tyrannida vocat, a ceteris prudentissime separavit.
Nam Persarum aut Turcorum imperium nihil commune
habet cum graecis italicisve civitatibus neque cum
christianis Europae gentibus.

At enim Tyrannis forma tantum Monarchiae est ; rex
enim, et in Monarchia, leges mutandi jus habet ; ergo
ipsius voluntas suprema lex est.[a] Notandum vero earum
societatum structuram omnino diversam esse : nempe,
in Tyrannide, ea diversitate caret quae Monarchiae
peculiaris est. Ceterum nil refert utrum rex in Monarchia leges mutandi jus habeat an non ; nam facultatem
reipsa non habet, propterea quod ordinum potestas
ipsius potestatem continet. Secundato quidem merito
objectum est tyrannorum imperium sine ullo modo
nusquam exstitisse.[1] Sed scriptor ipse primam quam
dederat definitionem emendavit et in ipsa quoque
Tyrannide quoddam esse summae potestatis tempera-
mentum agnovit, sed aliud atque in Monarchia. Etenim
non ex diversorum ordinum institutione oritur, sed e
summa et singulari auctoritate qua religio non modo
apud populum, sed etiam apud tyrannum fruitur.[2]

---

1. Janet, op. cit., II, 345. [b]

2. « C'est la religion qui corrige un peu la constitution turque. » (V,
14.) — « Il y a pourtant une chose que l'on peut quelquefois opposer à la
volonté du prince; c'est la religion. » (III, 10.) — « De là vient que, dans

understanding of how in Rome and Athens the possessions of each citizen were limited, which was why there was social unity. In contrast, in the modern world, private life has grown and has broader boundaries. We each have our own personality, opinions, morals, religion, and set ourselves and our affairs more thoroughly apart from society and public affairs. Therefore social cohesion cannot be the same or come from the same source, but depends on a division of labour which makes individuals and groups necessary to one another. Finally, he had great shrewdness in picking out and identifying "despotism" as a separate type from the rest. An empire like that of the Persians or the Turks has nothing in common with the Greek and Italian city-states, or with the Christian nations of Europe.

It might be objected that despotism is only a form of monarchy, since even in monarchy the king has the right to change the laws, and so his will is the supreme law.[a] But, it should be emphasized, the structure of these societies is completely different, since in despotism there is not the diversity that is characteristic of monarchy. Nor does it matter, in the case of monarchy, if the king does or does not have the right to change the laws; he does not have the ability to do so, since his power is checked by the power of the social orders. A legitimate criticism of Montesquieu is that there has never been such a thing as the absolute, unfettered rule of a tyrant.[1] But he himself corrected his original definition, to recognize a constraint on the ruler's power even in despotism, though it is not the same as in monarchy. Its source is not the institution of different social orders, but the extraordinary, absolute authority enjoyed by religion amongst the people, and with the ruler too.[2]

---

1. Janet, *op. cit.*, vol. II, 345. [b]

2. "It is religion that to some extent corrects the Turkish constitution." (V, 14) – "However, there is one thing which can sometimes be opposed to the ruler's will, and it is religion." (III, 10) – "This is why religion

Nec dubium est quin religio in iis societatibus eam vim revera habeat. Nam non modo a principis voluntate non pendet, sed contra princeps, ut noster bene animadvertit,[1] ab ea ipsa immanem suam potestatem accipit ; nil ergo mirum si ab eadem contineatur.

Si vero Secundati doctrinam his de rebus penitus intelligere velis, quartum genus prioribus addendum est quod ab interpretibus immerito omitti solet. Dignum autem est quod nos moretur, nam ex eo Monarchia exstitit.[2] Scilicet societates comprehendit quae venando aut pecora pascendo vivunt. A ceteris enim multis et eximiis rebus differunt : cives perpauci sunt;[3] terra inter eos non dividitur,[4] non legibus sed moribus reguntur,[5] senes apud eos maximam auctoritatem habent, sed libertatis tam studiosi sunt ut nullum stabile imperium patiantur.[6] Certum est eam esse gentium inferiorum naturam quae, ob hanc causam, Democratia inferior appellari possit. Hoc autem genus in duas varietates Secundatus dividit. Cum per parvas hujusmodi nationes homines separantur quae nulla societate inter se conjunguntur, feras gentes illas appellat ; barbaricas vero, si in unam coeunt.[7] Aliae venationem, aliae pastorum vitam potius colunt.

---

ces pays, la religion a ordinairement tant de force ; c'est qu'elle forme une espèce de dépôt et de permanence : et, si ce n'est pas la religion, ce sont les coutumes qu'on y vénère, au lieu des lois. [a] » (II, 4.)

1. « Dans les empires mahométans, c'est de la religion que les peuples tirent en partie le respect étonnant qu'ils ont pour leur prince. [b] » (V, 14.)

2. XI, 8.

3. XVIII, 10.

4. XVIII, 13.

5 *Ibid.*

6. XVIII, 14. [c]

7. XVIII, 11. [d]

There can be no doubt that in such societies religion really does have this force. Not only is it not dependent on the ruler's will, but, as Montesquieu sees so well,[1] it is itself the source of the ruler's enormous power. So there is nothing surprising about its limitation of this.

It is necessary for a thorough understanding of Montesquieu's approach on these matters to add a fourth type, undeservedly neglected by most commentators. It is important to notice, since it forms the origins of monarchy.[2] It consists of societies that live by hunting or pastoralism, and that differ from the others in many, quite striking ways – their population is very small;[3] land is not divided up amongst them;[4] they are ruled by custom rather than law;[5] it is the old who have most authority amongst them, but they are so attached to freedom that they do not tolerate fixed, established government.[6] It is clear that such things describe the nature of primitive peoples, and so it is possible to refer to primitive democracy. Montesquieu divides this type into two categories. He talks of "savage" peoples in the case of small, dispersed tribes that are not linked together in any way to form a society, and of "barbarians" if they combine and unite.[7] In general, the first live by hunting and the second are herdsmen.

---

generally has so much force in these countries: it forms a kind of permanent depository; and if it is not religion, it is customs that are venerated in place of the laws." (II, 4).

1. "In Muslim empires, it is partly from religion that the people derive the astonishing respect they have for their ruler." (V, 14).
2. XI, 8.
3. XVIII, 10.
4. XVIII, 13.
5. *Ibid.*
6. XVIII, 14. [c]
7. XVIII, 11. [d]

Societatem igitur divisio, qualem Secundatus esse concepit, sequenti tabula exprimitur:

Societates

Quae definitam summi imperii constitutionem habent......
Monarchia.
Respublica.
Tyrannis.[1]
Aristocratia.
Democratia.

Sine definita summi imperii constitutione................
Barbaricae gentes.
Ferae gentes.

Quicumque hanc tabulam ante oculos habet multasque illas populorum varietates quas comprehendit, Secundatum intelligit non Aristotelis divisionem paulo infidelius retulisse, sed aliquod novum instauravisse.

---

1. Quibus addendae sunt societates quae e pluribus populis, foedere conjunctis, constant. (IX, 1-3.)

Montesquieu's classification of societies is set out in the following table:

Societies

| With a clearly constituted government............. | { | Monarchy.
Republic.
Despotism.[1] | { | Aristocracy.
Democracy. |

| Without a clearly constituted government............. | { | Barbarian peoples.
Savage peoples. |

It is clear from this table and the many different societies covered by it that Montesquieu did not reproduce, with a few changes, Aristotle's classification, but that he established a new one.

---

1. To which should be added societies that consist of many peoples, joined in a federation (IX, 1-3).

CAPUT QUARTUM

QUATENUS POLITICARUM RERUM LEGES CERTAS ESSE SECUNDATUS SENSERIT

I

Age vero; non solum societates per genera dividit, sed politica facta ac praesertim ea de quibus praecipue loquitur, leges scilicet, ordinem certum sequi rationalique igitur interpretationi idonea esse existimat. Hoc jam apparet e libri initio ubi praeclaram illam legum definitionem invenies : Leges sunt necessariae connexiones quae ex rerum natura sequuntur.[a] Hoc enim non modo naturae leges, sed et eas quibus humanae societates reguntur comprehendit.

Comte quidem Secundatum criminatus est quasi ab hoc principio postea ita declinasset ut in rerum multitudine, quae in reliquo opere accumulantur, nullus ordo reperiri possit.[1] Haec autem accusatio a veritate recedit. Etenim quotiescumque de lege aliqua agitur, eam a certis conditionibus pendentem nobis ostendit. Duo sunt autem illarum conditionum genera. Aliae naturae rerum quas lex spectat inhaerent ; scilicet, si ad commercium pertinet, commercii naturae, si vero ad religionem, religionis. Est autem alia causa quae suam vim multo latius extendit ceterisque praevalet ; id est natura societatis. Pleraeque enim leges, ut jam diximus, non eaedem esse possunt in Monarchia atque

---

1. *Cours de phil. pos.*, IV, 181. [b]

CHAPTER FOUR

THE EXTENT TO WHICH MONTESQUIEU SAW
DEFINITE LAWS OF THE POLITICAL WORLD

I

Montesquieu not only divides societies into types, but considers that political facts and especially those he talks of most – namely, laws – follow a definite order and so are open to rational explanation. This is apparent right from the beginning of his book, where we find the famous definition: "Laws are the necessary connexions which follow from the nature of things".[a] This covers, not just laws of nature, but those by which human societies are governed.

Comte attacked Montesquieu on the grounds that he afterwards departed from this principle to such an extent that it is impossible to discover any order in the mass of facts piled up in the rest of the work.[1] The accusation has little to do with the truth. Whenever he considers a law he shows us that it depends on definite conditions. These are of two kinds. Some are inherent in the nature of the things with which the law is concerned – the nature of commerce, for example, if it is a law about commerce, or of religion if it is about religion. But there is another cause which extends its influence much more widely and dominates the rest; this is the nature of society. As we have already said, it is impossible for most laws to be the same

---

1. *Course of Positive Philosophy,* IV, 181. [b]

in Republica aut in Tyrannide ; denique in gentibus inferioribus omnino desunt. Itaque fac populum unius aut alterius generis esse, unus omnium legum tenor necessario sequitur.

Quin Secundatus causarum effectuumque seriem etiam longius repetit. Non modo demonstrat leges e societatis forma pendere, sed et causas e quibus ipsae societatum formae pendent inquirit ; inter quas primas partes tenet societatis amplitudo.

Finge enim societatem in angustos fines contractam; nemo est quin res communes ante oculos continuo habeat et animo amplectatur. Praeterea, cum vitae conditiones omnibus eaedem ferme sint — nam in tali civitate spatium ipsum diversitati deest — et vivendi ratio non varia esse potest ; etiam qui gubernaculum tenent, propterea quod parva potestate, pro populi parvitate, instruuntur, nihil aliud sunt quam primi inter pares. Patriae igitur imago non modo omnium menti obversatur, sed maximam vim habet quia nulla alia continetur.[1] Ex hac descriptione Reipublicae naturam agnoscis.[2] Si vero societas crescit, omnia mutantur. Nam commune bonum sentire privato cuique civi jam difficilius est, quippe qui publicarum rerum exiguam tantum partem adspiciat. Circumstantiae praeterea, cum multo magis diversae sint, singulos impellunt ut alii alio tendant et ferantur in diversa. Adde summam auctoritatem tantam effici ut, qui eam exercet, ceteris longe superemineat.[3] Itaque ex Republica societas in

---

1. « Dans une petite (république), le bien public est mieux senti, mieux connu, plus près de chaque citoyen. » (VIII, 16.)

2. « Il est de la nature de la république qu'elle n'ait qu'un petit territoire; sans cela, elle ne peut guère subsister. » (*Ibid.*)

3. « Dans une grande république, il y a de grandes fortunes [...]: il y a de trop grands dépôts à mettre entre les mains d'un citoyen ; les intérêts se particularisent. » (*Ibid.*) [a]

in a monarchy as in a republic or under despotism, and there are not any amongst primitive peoples. Given the type of society, a single tendency of all the laws necessarily follows.

Indeed, Montesquieu traces the sequence of causes and effects even further back. He not only shows that laws depend on the form of society, but investigates the causes on which forms of society themselves depend: amongst these the size of society has first place.

Think of a society confined within narrow limits. There is not anyone not immediately aware of communal affairs and preoccupied by them. Moreover, since the conditions of life are almost the same for all – the very room for diversity is lacking in such a community – there also cannot be variation in lifestyle. Even those in government, having limited power in line with the limits of the people, are only first amongst equals. The idea of country is not only present to everyone's mind, but has the greatest force because it is not constrained by any other.[1] We can recognize from this description the nature of a republic.[2] But if society becomes larger everything is changed. It is more difficult for the private citizen to have a sense of the common good, since each is aware of only a small part of public affairs. Circumstances are much more diverse, forcing individuals to go different ways and become involved in different things. And the power of the state is so great that whoever exercises it stands far above all others.[3] In this way society necessarily changes from a

---

1. "In a small (republic), the public good is better felt, better known, and closer to each citizen." (VIII, 16).

2 "It is in the nature of a republic to have only a small territory; otherwise, it can scarcely continue to exist." (*Ibid.*)

3. "In a large republic, there are large fortunes [...]: the stores are too large to put in the hands of one citizen; interests become particularized." (*Ibid.*) [a]

Monarchiam necessario evadit.[1] Si vero non modo modestam, sed nimiam amplitudinem habet, Monarchia abit in Tyrannida. Nam vastum imperium non stare possit nisi princeps absolutam potestatem habeat qua tot populos tanto spatio dispersos contineat.[2] Adeo arcta est ea connexio inter naturam societatum earumdemque amplitudinem ut cujusque principium pereat si populus ultra modum crescit aut contra minuitur.[3]

Sane multa sunt in iis quae redargui debeant. Etenim innumeri sunt populi qui, quanquam mediocrem aut etiam exiguam amplitudinem habent, sub tyrannis vivunt. Alii contra, ut Judaeorum gens, quamvis graecas italicasque civitates magnitudine longe exsuperaverint, quamdam tamen Democratiae formam praebuerunt. Praeterea in ipsa explicatione, si in singula descenderis, non nihil incerti vagique saepius reperies. Nihilominus ingenui sui acumen Secundatus ostendit cum civium numero tantum pondus attribuit. Ea enim causa maximam vim habet ad res politicas definiendas ; quin eam quasi fontem esse credimus ex quo praecipuae differentiae inter societates ortae sunt. Prout incolae pauci sunt aut contra numerosi, religio, familia, mores, jus, etc., non eadem esse possunt. Hoc unum Secundatum latuit non civium numerum qui sub eadem auctoritate rediguntur referre, sed eorum qui commercio aliquo conjunguntur. Nam quamvis multi eidem principi pareant, si alii ab aliis ita distant ut

---

1. « Un état monarchique doit être d'une grandeur médiocre. S'il était petit, il se formerait en république. » (VIII, 17.)

2. « Un grand empire suppose une autorité despotique dans celui qui gouverne. » (VIII, 19.)

3. « Il suit que, pour conserver le principe du gouvernement établi, il faut maintenir l'État dans la grandeur qu'il avait déjà. » (VIII, 20).

republic into monarchy.[1] But if it is very great, rather than only moderate in size, monarchy turns into despotism. This is because it is impossible for a large empire to survive unless its ruler has the absolute power to hold in check many peoples spread over a vast land.[2] The connexion between the nature of a society and its size is so close that its principle is lost if there is an excessive increase or fall in population.[3]

Of course, much of all this may be refuted. There are innumerable peoples who, although moderate or even small in number, live under tyrants. Others, such as the Jewish nation, although far larger than the Greek and Italian city-states, involved a form of democracy. Moreover, in the explanation itself, when we get down to details we quite often find things that are uncertain and vague. Even so, Montesquieu shows his intellectual sharpness in attributing such importance to the number of citizens. This cause has the greatest influence in determining things in the political world, and indeed we believe it is more or less the source from which the main differences between societies arise. Depending on whether these have few or many people living in them, religion, the family, morals, law, etc., cannot be the same. The one point to escape Montesquieu is that it is not the number of those brought under the same authority which matters, but the number of those brought together in some sort of interchange. Even though there are many people under the same ruler, if they are so distant from one another that there

---

1. "A monarchical state should be of medium size. If it were small, it would form itself into a republic." (VIII, 17).

2. "A large empire presupposes a despotic authority in the one who governs." (VIII, 19).

3. "It follows that, in order to preserve the principles of the established government, the state must be maintained at the size it already has." (VIII, 20).

nulla aut rara tantum commercia inter eos existere possint, eorum copia nullius effectus est.

Ceterum, praeter hanc causam, plures alias Secundatus addit quae per se nonnihil valent ad societates
constituendas. Eae sunt de quibus interpretes praecipue
disseruerunt. Sic natura soli, si in vastis continuisque
campis consistit, Tyrannidis institutioni favet propterea
quod magna imperia ibi facilius sese possunt extendere.
Montana contra aut insulae libertatis arces sunt quia
principis auctoritas montibus aut oceano quasi frangi-
tur.[1] Non modo terrae forma, sed ipsius natura consi-
deranda est. Quaedam sterilitas, cum animos ad labo-
rem et frugalitatem impellat, Reipublicae viam aperit;
fertilitas contra, quae divitiarum amorem privataeque
utilitatis curam excitat, Monarchiae ;[2] si vero nimia
est, gentium inferiorum Democratiae.[3] Nam terrae,
cum sponte fructus edant, non coluntur ideoque inter
cives non dividuntur. Denique caeli calor animos et corpora
effeminat hominesque ad servitutem cogit.[4]

Ex iisdem vero causis non modo natura societatis et
inde totum jus summatim pro parte pendet, sed et
peculiares quaedam leges tales efficiuntur quales sunt.
Sic nimius caeli ardor servorum ad privatos usus institutionem[5] et jus plures feminas habendi[6] multosque
domesticos mores[7] suscitat. Praeterea mentis corporisque segnities, quae inde sequitur, leges, religiones,

---

1. XVII, 6, et XVIII, 5.
2. XVIII, 1 et 2.
3. XVIII, 9 et sq.
4. XVII, 2.
5. XV, 7.
6. XVI, 2.
7. XVI, 10.

can be little or no contact between them their numbers have no effect.

There are many other causes that Montesquieu brings in besides this, each contributing something to the way societies are formed. It is these that commentators mostly discuss. A country of vast open plains favours the establishment of despotism, since the growth of large empires becomes easier. But mountainous regions and islands are strongholds of freedom, since mountains and the sea break up a ruler's power.[1] And it is necessary to consider, not just the terrain, but the nature of the land itself. If it is not very productive, people have to be hard-working and frugal, thus opening the way to a republic. If it is fertile, it stirs up love of wealth and concern for self-interest, opening the way to monarchy.[2] Abundance, however, leads to primitive democracy.[3] Lands that yield up their fruits spontaneously are not cultivated and so are not divided out amongst individuals. Finally, a hot climate enervates body and mind, forcing men into slavery.[4]

The same causes not only help to determine the nature of society and so, very generally, the entire law. They affect, too, the substance of particular laws. A very hot climate leads to the institution of slaves for private use,[5] the right to several wives,[6] and many customs of domestic life,[7] while the intellectual and physical torpor resulting from it produces the static character of law, morals and

1. XVII, 6, and XVIII, 5.
2. XVIII, 1 and 2.
3. XVIII, 9 et *sq.*
4. XVII, 2.
5. XV, 7.
6. XVI, 2.
7. XVI, 10.

mores immobiles efficit.[1] Ex iisdem causis commercii natura alia est in Oriente atque in Europa.[2]

Quamvis has causas non pari linea atque priorem posuerit ac praevalere tantum apud feras gentes ipse agnoverit,[3] fatendum est tamen earum vim nusquam tantam fuisse quantam judicavit. Domestica enim et politica privataque virtus in regionibus, quae caeli terraeque natura longissime differunt, aeque occurrit. Sed, quidquid id est, hoc ipsum ostendit quantum Secundatus senserit res politicas legibus certis subditas esse. Etenim omnia haec, si in breve coguntur, huc redeunt : ex populi cujusdam magnitudine, ex soli forma quod idem occupet, ex terrae caelique natura deduci posse cujus generis sit illa societas et quae sint hujus leges et instituta.

Sed unam tantum doctrinae partem, quam Secundatus in suo libro exposuit, adhuc retulimus. Aliam nunc videamus quae priori contraria esse videtur. Haec contradictio digna est quam penitus inspiciamus. Ex ea enim melius intelligetur non modo quae sit integra scriptoris nostri sententia, sed etiam quae difficultates, Secundati saeculo atque etiam nostro tempore, politicae scientiae institutioni obstiterint.

II

Quicumque, ut supra vidimus, in politica vita ordinem certum esse existimat, legislatoris partes necessario elevat. Nam civilia instituta, si e rerum natura sequuntur, non ex unius civis aut plurium voluntate pendent.

---

1. XIV, 4.

2. XXI, 1.

3. « La nature et le climat dominent presque seuls sur les sauvages. » (XIX, 4.) [a]

religion.[1] It is due to the same causes that the nature of commerce is different in the East and in Europe.[2]

But although, in his view, these are less important causes than the others and predominate, on his own admission, only amongst savage peoples,[3] it has to be said that their influence has never been as great as he thought. There are similar morals of family and private and public life in countries with a completely different climate and geography. Even so, all this goes to show the extent to which Montesquieu regarded the political world as subject to definite laws. If we sum up everything so far, it comes down to this: given the number of people in a society, the form of terrain it occupies and the nature of the land and climate, it is possible to deduce what type of society it is and what laws and institutions it has.

But we have gone over, up until now, only one part of the approach which Montesquieu set out in his book. Let us turn to look, at this point, at another, which seems at odds with it. The contradiction is worth examining as throroughly as possible. It gives us a better understanding not only of Montesquieu's thought as a whole, but of difficulties, in his own time and ours, blocking the development of political science.

II

As we have already seen, recognition of a definite order in political life necessarily reduces the role of the legislator. Social institutions, if following from the nature of things, do not depend on the will of one individual or of many.

1. XIV, 4.
2. XXI, 1.
3. "Nature and climate rule almost alone over savages." (XIX, 4).

Contra, apud Secundatum, legislatoris persona manifesto ita eminet ut tanquam necessarius legum artifex appareat. In multis operis locis, de Romanorum, Spartanorum, Atheniensium legibus ita loquitur quasi a Romulo aut Numa, a Solone, a Lycurgo creatae fuissent.[1] Cum, in alio libro, primas Romanae civitatis origines enarrat, tanquam principium statuit, populorum nascentium instituta a principibus fieri et posterius tantum principes ex institutis instrui.[2] Hoc est cur leges a moribus omnino separet ; mores enim e communi vita sponte nascuntur, leges contra sine peculiari quadam legislatoris institutione existere nequeunt.[3] Is est hujus sententiae sensus quam in primo libri capite invenies : « Quanquam ad societatem nati, homines publica sua officia oblivisci poterant nisi ad ea a legislatoribus revocati fuissent. »[4] [b] Sane leges de omni re et ad libitum creari posse non credit ; sed mores et religionem extra legislatoris potestatem esse arbitratur et leges ipsas quae de aliis rebus feruntur moribus et religioni accommodandas esse.[5] Nihilominus earum institutio in legislatoris manu versatur. Immo sunt societates in quibus non leges tantum, sed et religio moresque a principe informari possunt.[6] Quanquam hoc in raris

---

1. « Je prie qu'on fasse un peu d'attention à l'étendue de génie qu'il fallut à ces législateurs pour voir qu'en choquant tous les usages reçus... ils montreraient à l'univers leur sagesse. » (IV, 6. [a] Cf. V, 5, et XIX, 16.)

2. « Dans la naissance des sociétés, ce sont les chefs des républiques qui font l'institution ; et c'est ensuite l'institution qui forme les chefs des républiques. » (*Grandeur et Décadence des Romains*, chap. I.)

3. « Les lois sont établies, les moeurs sont inspirées ; celles-ci tiennent plus à l'esprit général, celles-là tiennent plus à une institution particulière. » (XIX, 12.) — « Nous avons dit que les lois étaient des institutions particulières et précises du législateur, [et] les moeurs et les manières des institutions de la nation en général. » (XIX, 14.)

4. *In fine.*

5. XIX, 21.

6. XIX, 16 et 19.

But with Montesquieu the part of the legislator is so important that he appears as the indispensable architect of the laws. There are many passages in his work where he talks about the laws of the Romans, Spartans and Athenians as if they were created by Romulus and Numa, Solon, and Lycurgus.[1] In an account, in another book, of the origins of the Roman state, he set down, as a principle, that the institutions of newly forming societies are made by the leaders and it is only later that the leaders are shaped by the institutions.[2] This is why he sees laws as altogether distinct from morals: morals develop spontaneously from communal life, but laws cannot exist without the special decree of a legislator. This is the sense of the claim found in the first chapter of the book: "Although born for society, men can forget their public duties unless brought back to them by legislators".[4] [b] Of course, he does not believe that laws can be created at will and about anything. He considers that morals and religion are beyond the power of the legislator and that even laws on other matters must be adapted to morals and religion.[5] But the institution of these is still in the hands of the legislator. Indeed, there are societies in which the ruler is able to shape not just laws but also morals and religion.[6] Although there are

---

1. "I pray for a little attention to the extensive genius necessary for those legislators to see that in upsetting all received usages... they would show the universe their wisdom." (IV, 6. [a] Cf. V, 5, and XIX, 16).

2. "When societies start up, the leaders of republics make the system of institutions, and later on the system of institutions shapes the leaders of republics." (*The Grandeur and Decadence of the Romans*, ch. 1).

3. "Laws are established, morals are inspired; the latter depend more on the general spirit, the former depend more on a particular institution." (XIX, 12) – "We have said that laws were particular and precise institutions of the legislator, morals and manners institutions of the nation in general." (XIX, 14).

4. Conclusion.

5. XIX, 21.

6. XIX, 16 and 19.

tantum casibus occurrit, eo tamen monstratur quantum, ex Secundato, valeat principis auctoritas.

Facile intelliges unde hoc venerit si modo perspexeris quo sensu Secundatus dixerit leges humanas e rerum natura sequi. Sententia enim per se ambigua est et duplicem interpretationem patitur. Aut leges e rerum, id est e societatum natura necessario oriuntur ut effectus e causa quae eum gignit ; aut media quaedam tantummodo sunt quae societatis natura requirit ut ipsa absolvatur, id est ad finem suum perveniat ; quibus tamen carere potest.[a] Aliis verbis, utrum intelligendum est societatis statum legum causam efficientem esse, an earumdem causam tantummodo finalem ? Priorem autem sensum ne suspicari quidem videtur Secundatus. Non dicit ex paucitate civium, ineluctabili quadam necessitate, Democratiae leges nasci tanquam calorem ex igne, sed eas solas esse quibus frugalitas et omnium aequalitas, quae in hujusmodi societatis natura est, ad effectum adduci queat. Ceterum non ideo leges ex libidine fabricari possunt ; nam, datis quibusdam populi conditionibus, unum legum corpus est quod ei conveniat nec ullum aliud imponi possit sine societatis corruptione. Sed ut provideatur quid genti cuique congruat, necesse est homines esse qui acuto ingenio rerum naturam scrutentur et quo tendi debeat et qua via dispiciant. Hoc est legislatorum munus ; nil mirum igitur si Secundatus primatum quemdam illis attribuerit. Finge contra leges e causis efficientibus oriri quarum etiam homines saepius inconscii sunt, legislatoris officia jam minuuntur ; nam in eo tantum consistunt ut, quod in ceteris conscientiis obscurius latet, manifestius exprimat. Sed nihil aut fere nihil novum excogitat ; immo, etiamsi absit, nihil impedit quin leges exstent quanquam minus definitae. Sane non scribi possunt nisi per legislatorem ;

only rare cases of this, it brings out how much influence a ruler's authority has for Montesquieu.

It is easy to understand the source of this view once we examine the sense of Montesquieu's statement, that human laws follow from the nature of things. In itself it is ambiguous, allowing two interpretations. Either laws arise necessarily from the nature of things, that is, of societies, as an effect arises from the cause producing it. Or they are only means which the nature of society requires to realize itself, that is, to achieve its end; but these might be lacking.[a] In other words, is the state of society to be understood as the efficient cause of the laws, or just as their final cause? Montesquieu seems not even to suspect the first sense. He does not say that democracy's laws result from low population size with an unavoidable necessity, like heat from fire, but that it is only through them that there can come about the frugalness and general equality which lie in the nature of this society. It does not at all follow from this that laws can be made arbitrarily. There is one set of laws suited to a people, given their circumstances, and it is impossible to impose any other without corruption of the society. But to provide for what suits each people, there must be persons with the insight and intelligence to examine the nature of things and see where and in what way it must develop. This is the job of legislators; so it is not surprising if Montesquieu gave them a certain preeminence. On the assumption, instead, that laws arise from efficient causes and that people are quite often unaware of these, the role of the legislator becomes less important. All it involves is giving clearer expression to what is hidden and more obscure in the minds of the others. He does not think up much if anything new. Even if he did not exist, there is nothing to stop there being laws, if less well defined. Of course, only the

hic autem instrumentum potius est quo instituantur quam earum causa generatrix.

Non hic locus est disputandi num sint civilia instituta quae a causis finalibus tota pendeant ; at certe non dubium est ea rarissima esse. Etenim politica vita tot tantaque in se continet ut nemo eam animo amplecti valeat ; itaque non facile est quid eidem profuturum sit, quid non, praevidere. Etiamsi haec computatio mentem humanam plerumque non exsuperet, adeo abstrusa est ut non magnam vim habere possit ad voluntates movendas. Res igitur civiles non ex ratione constituta fieri solent ; leges non media sunt quae legislator excogitat propterea quod societatis naturae concinere videntur ; sed e causis saepissime nascuntur quae eas gignunt physica quadam necessitate. Ex conditionibus in quibus versatur populus communis vita ita efficitur ut formam quamdam definitam necessario induat ; leges autem hanc formam exprimunt ; ex iisdem igitur efficientibus causis eadem necessitate sequuntur. Si vero hoc infitieris, tum accipiendum sit plerasque res politicas et praesertim eas quae majoris momenti sint, omnino sine causis esse. Nullus enim unquam homo exstitit qui ex parva Romae nascentis amplitudine leges, quae tali populo convenirent, deduxerit; aequalitatem et frugalitatem, quam illae e Secundato praecipiebant, non ipsae creaverunt, sed, ex ea ipsa ortae, eamdem tantum confirmavere.

Hoc sane sensisset Secundatus si perspexisset leges a moribus non natura distare, sed contra ab iis emanare.[1]

---

1. Sane legislatorem jubet populi mores et ingenium sequi (XIX, 2-6) legesque demonstrat quamdam vim habere ad mores informandos (XIX, 27). Ea tamen ita separat ut quod legibus institutum est et legibus tantum mutari posse censeat, moribus vero quod ad mores attinet (XIX, 14). Inde fit ut non facile intellexerit quo modo omnia haec apud quosdam populos confusa sint. (XIX, 16 et sq.)

52

legislator can write them down, but he is the instrument of their establishment rather than the originating cause.

This is not the place to discuss if social institutions exist that depend entirely on final causes. At least we can be sure there are very few. Political life involves so many important things that nobody can grasp it all. As a result it is not easy to look ahead to see what would work for the good, and what would not. Even if it is not a calculation largely beyond the human mind, it is so abstract it can have little power to move the will. Thus social institutions do not usually become established according to a plan, and laws are not devices a legislator invents because they seem in line with the nature of a society. They are most often the result of causes that produce them with something like a physical necessity. Collective life is so shaped by a people's circumstances that it must take on a particular definite form. The laws express this form. They therefore follow from the same efficient causes with the same necessity. If this is denied it then has to be accepted that most things in the political world – and especially the more important – have no causes at all. No individual ever existed who might have deduced, from the small size of early Rome, the laws suited to such a society. These did not create the frugalness and equality which, according to Montesquieu, they taught, but arose from that way of life itself and merely reinforced it.

Montesquieu would undoubtedly have realized this if he had seen that laws are not so different in nature from morals, but, on the contrary, emanate from them.[1]

---

1. True, he instructs the legislator to work in line with the morality and temperament of a people (XIX, 2-6), and brings out how laws have some influence over morals (XIX, 27). They remain in his view so distinct that what is established by laws can be changed only by laws, what relates to morals, only by morals (XIX, 14). Hence his difficulty in understanding how, in some societies, these all merged. (XIX, 16 *et sq.*)

Nam nihil aliud sunt quam mores melius definiti ; mores autem nemo nescit non consulto institui, sed causis quae suos effectus, insciis ipsis hominibus, edunt generari. Itaque non alia est plerarumque legum origo. Non tamen ideo utilitate carent ; contra non durare possent nisi quas utiles partes in societate tenerent. Sed non hujus utilitatis causa natae sunt ; quae contra vulgo ignoratur, nedum provisa sit. Sentimus enim juris aut morum regulas bonas esse, sed, cum interrogamur quo pertineant, sine fine disputatur. Sin igitur quaerere licet qua ratione lex aliqua societati prosit, non ideo explicatur unde ea venerit. Itaque, qui politicarum rerum finales causas unice indagatur, mancam scientiam effingit, quippe quem earumdem origines lateant. Ea autem erit politica scientia si Secundati methodum sequemur.

III

Quin etiam non modo juris regulae e societatis natura non necessario sequuntur, quippe quae in rebus absconditae latere queant, nisi quis legislator eas adspiciat et in lucem edat, sed et aliam formam ex Secundato habere possunt quam quae e causis, a quibus pendent, sequitur. Humanis enim societatibus nescio quam facultatem attribuit a sua ipsarum natura declinandi : leges naturales, quae suae constitutioni inhaerent, homines non eadem necessitate sequantur qua res inanimatae, sed jugum interdum excutere valeant.[1] Rebus igitur politicis *contingentiam* supponit quae,

---

1. « Mais il s'en faut bien que le monde intelligent soit aussi bien gouverné que le monde physique. Car, quoique celui-là ait aussi des lois qui, par leur nature, sont invariables, il ne les suit pas constamment comme le monde physique suit les siennes. » (I, 1.)

They are only morals and customs more precisely defined, and these, as everyone knows, are not a deliberate creation but lie in causes that produce their effects without people themselves realizing it. The origin of most laws is the same. It does not follow that they lack usefulness. On the contrary, they cannot remain in existence without a useful function in society. But they do not come into existence because of this usefulness, which is usually not understood, still less aimed at and foreseen. We sense that the rules of law and morality are good, yet when we are asked what they are for there is endless dispute. We can still to try to work out how a law benefits society. But this is not to explain its source. Investigating only the final causes of things in the political world constructs a defective science, losing sight of their origins. This is what political science would be like if we followed Montesquieu's method.

III

It is not just that the rules of law do not necessarily follow from the nature of society, since they can lie concealed in things unless a legislator sees and brings them to light. It is also that for Montesquieu they can have a different form from the one which follows from the causes on which they depend. He gives human societies a mysterious power to deviate from their own nature: men need not follow the natural laws, inherent in their condition, with the same necessity as inanimate things, but can sometimes throw off the yoke.[1] He therefore introduces into the political world a *contingency* which

---

1. "But the intelligent world is far from being as well governed as the physical world. For although it also has laws that are invariable by their nature, unlike the physical world it does not always follow them." (I, 1).

primo quidem adspectu, cum ordinis certi existentia non coire posse videtur ; namque, si ita se res haberet, connexiones inter causas et effectus non constantes nec immotae manerent. Itaque refert quae sit haec contingentia definire ; nam valde timendum est ne fundamenta ipsa politicae scientiae eruat.

Forsitan in mentem tibi veniet Secundatum hanc contingentiam statuisse quia, ea sublata, et humana libertas tolli videatur. At, si hanc causam vere haberet, sine ulla exceptione esset et totam vitam amplecteretur. Mirum autem esset scriptorem nostrum a se ipso ita dissensisse, quippe qui homines et societates legibus regi tam expressis verbis declaraverit easque reperire tentaverit. Praeterea minime verisimile est hujus doctrinam quacumque metaphysica fundatum esse. Nihil est enim in toto opere quod aliquam metaphysicarum quaestionum curam ostendat ; nusquam de libero arbitrio agitur. Itaque non est cur haec philosophorum hypothesis tantam apud eum vim habuerit. Ceterum est in primo libri capite locus qui hanc interpretationem manifesto refellit. Nam Secundatus hanc contingentiam non hominis propriam esse dicit, sed eamdem et in ceteris animalibus reperit, immo in plantis ipsis omnino non abesse existimare videtur.[1]

Ipse nos monet se hanc contingentiam tantummodo excogitavisse ut errores unde existant explicare posset.[2] Si enim nunquam erraremus, naturae nostrae

---

1. « (Les bêtes) ont des lois naturelles, parce qu'elles sont unies par le sentiment... Elles ne suivent pas pourtant invariablement leurs lois naturelles : les plantes, en qui nous ne remarquons ni connaisance ni sentiment, les suivent mieux. » (I, 1.)

2. « Il s'en faut [bien] que le monde intelligent soit aussi bien gouverné que le monde physique... La raison en est que les êtres particuliers intelligents sont bornés par leur nature, et par conséquent sujets à l'erreur ; et, d'un autre côté, il est de leur nature qu'ils agissent par euxmêmes. » (I, 1. Cf. ejusdem capitis finem.)

seems, at least at first sight, incompatible with the existence of a definite order, since it implies that relations of cause and effect would not remain stable and fixed. So it is important to sort out what, exactly, this contingency is, because of a genuine fear that it may destroy the very foundations of political science.

It might be thought that Montesquieu insisted on contingency since, with its elimination, human freedom seems eliminated too. But if these were the real grounds, it would apply without exception and cover all of life. It would be surprising if Montesquieu contradicted himself in this way, since he is so explicit that men and societies are governed by laws and set out to discover these. And it is highly improbable that his approach had any basis in metaphysics. There is no sign, in the entire work, of a concern with metaphysical issues – or a discussion, anywhere, of freewill. So there is no saying why this philosophical hypothesis should have had so great an importance for him. Moreover, there is a passage in the book's first chapter which clearly refutes such an interpretation. Montesquieu says that the contingency he has in mind is not special to men; he finds it in all other animals, and even seems to suppose it is not altogether absent in plants.[1]

He himself informs us that the only reason he thought of contingency was to be able to explain how errors come about[2] – if we never erred, we would follow the laws of

---

1. "(The beasts) have natural laws because they are united by feeling... Still, they do not invariably follow their natural laws: plants, in which we observe neither knowledge nor feeling, follow theirs better." (I, 1).

2. "But the intelligent world is far from being as well governed as the physical world... The reason for this is that particular intelligent beings are limited by their nature and consequently subject to error; and, on the other hand, it is in their nature to act by themselves." (I, 1. *Cf.* the end of the same chapter.)

leges in omni occasione sequeremur. Si vero intelligere velis quid Secundatum ad hanc opinionem adduxerit, primum ponendum est quid per rerum naturam significet. Eo autem verbo designat non omnes alicujus rei proprietates, sed eas tantum quae ceteras in se contineant et rem faciant unius aut alterius generis esse,[1] [a] id est hujus essentiam. Praeterea logicum quoddam vinculum esse putat inter hanc naturam normalesque rei formas, ita ut eae priori implicentur. Itaque si homines et populi naturae suae nunquam derogent, semper et ubique erunt quales esse debent. Sunt autem in privata politicaque vita imperfecta multa ; sunt iniquae leges, vitiosae institutiones quas societates e legislatorum erroribus acceperunt. Omnia haec humanam quamdam facultatem a naturae legibus aberrandi significare Secundato videntur. Non ideo causis carent ; causae autem illae fortuitae sunt et, ut ita dicam, adventiciae.[2] [b] Non igitur ad leges reduci queunt ; rerum enim corrumpunt naturam quam contra leges exprimunt.

Sane principium, a quo tota haec argumentatio pendet, falsum est. Isti enim errores, quatenus ad civilem vitam attinent, nihil aliud sunt nisi corporis politici morbi; morbus autem animantium naturae non minus inest quam bona valetudo. Haec ergo non inter se contraria sunt, sed contra ejusdem generis, ita ut comparari possint et ex ea comparatione utriusque interpretatio proficiat. Sed haec falsa opinio cum externa rerum specie tam bene congruit ut etiam in physiologia diu permanserit. Nempe quia manifestum esse videtur animantes natura sanos esse, inde concluditur morbum, propterea quod valetudini obstat, vitae naturam violare.

---

1. « Il y a cette différence entre la nature du gouvernement et son principe, que sa nature est ce qui le fait être tel. » (III, 1.)

2. V. VIII, 10.

of our nature at all times. If we want to understand what led him to this idea a first task is to sort out what he means by the nature of things. He designates by this term, not all the properties of a thing, but only those which contain, in themselves, all the others, and which determine the particular kind of thing it is [1] [a] – that is, its essence. And he believes there is a logical connexion between the normal forms of a thing and its nature, such that these are implicit in it. If men and societies always lived up to their nature, then in all places and times they would be as they should be. In fact, both private and public life are far from perfect: there are unjust laws and pernicious institutions, that societies owe to the mistakes of legislators. Such things all seem evidence, in Montesquieu's view, of a human power to deviate from the laws of nature. It is not that they do not then have causes. Instead, their causes are accidental and, as one might say, external.[2] [b] They are therefore irreducible to laws, a corruption of the nature of things that laws, on the contrary, express.

The principle on which the whole argument depends is, of course, mistaken. The errors he talks about, in that they concern social life, are simply diseases of the political organism. And disease, as much as health, is part of the nature of a living being – so that, far from being opposites, they are of the same type. They can then be compared, and explanation of both develops through the comparison. But it is a mistake which fits the outward appearance of things well enough for it to have been a long-held and persistent view, even in physiology. It seems obvious that living beings are by nature healthy, leading to the conclusion that disease, since opposed to health, violates the nature of life.

---

1. "There is this difference between the nature of the government and its principle, that its nature is that which makes it what it is." (III, 1).

2. See VIII, 10.

Itaque jam Aristoteles morbos et monstra omnesque enormes vitae formas esse fructus obscurae cujusdam contingentiae arbitrabatur.[1] Scientia igitur politica statim ab isto errore liberari non poterat, praesertim cum morbus majorem locum nusquam teneat quam in humanis societatibus, normalisque status nusquam incertior sit ac difficilius definiatur.

Sic plures loci explanantur ubi Secundatus legislatorem mira quadam potestate instruere videtur naturae ipsi vim inferendi. In regionibus, exempli gratia, ubi nimius solis ardor ad nimiam pigritiam incolas invitat, legislatorem jubet eam omni via compescere.[2] At quamvis hoc vitium e causis physicis oriatur, tamen qui ei obstat naturam non violare nostro videtur, sed contra homines ad normalem ipsorum naturam revocare quae tantam segnitiem non patitur.[3] Eamdem ob causam apud feroces populos terribiles poenas instituere necessarium esse dicit ut haec morum ferocitas comprimatur.[4] In omnibus istis casibus legislator tantam potentiam habet non quod societates legibus ac natura definita careant ideoque ad libitum componi possint ; sed contra quia secundum normalem hominum societatumque naturam agit eique tantum auxiliatur.

Haec doctrina igitur non mera expressaque contradictione inficitur. Secundatus enim non iisdem politicis factis ordinem certum inesse eumdemque deesse dicit ; sed, ubicumque res justae sunt, secundum leges necessarias fiunt eaque necessitas tantummodo cessat cum

---

1. Zeller, *Philosophie der Griechen,* tertia editio, II, pars secunda, p.333. [a]

2. XIV, 6. [b]

3. « Quand donc la puissance physique de certains climats viole la loi naturelle..., c'est au législateur à faire des lois civiles qui forcent la nature du climat et rétablissent les lois primitives. » (XVI, 12.)

4. « Le peuple japonais a un caractère si atroce, que ses législateurs et ses magistrats n'ont pu avoir aucune confiance en lui : ils ne lui ont mis devant les yeux que des juges, des menaces et des châtiments. » (XIV, 15.) [c]

Aristotle therefore thought that disease along with grotesque and all abnormal forms of life are due to some obscure contingency.[1] Political science could not free itself of the error all at once, especially since disease has a greater place in human societies than anywhere else and the normal state is more uncertain and difficult to define.

This explains several passages in which Montesquieu seems to give the legislator a strange power to force nature itself into line. For example, in discussing countries where the extreme heat induces in people an extreme lethargy, he tells the legislator to do everything to limit this failing.[2] Thus the failing results from physical causes, yet the stand against it does not, in his view, violate nature, but instead takes men back to their normal nature, which rules out such inactivity.[3] For the same reason he says it is necessary to institute terrible punishments amongst a fierce people, to curb the fierceness of their ways.[4] In all these cases the legislator has such great power, not because societies lack laws and a definite nature and so can be constructed at will, but because he acts in line with the normal nature of men and societies and merely reinforces it.

Thus the approach is not vitiated by a simple, clearcut contradiction. Montesquieu does not say, of the same political facts, that there is a definite order in them and that there is not this. His view is that wherever things are as they should be they occur according to necessary laws, and this necessity ceases only when there is a deviation

---

1. Zeller, *Philosophy of the Greeks*, 3rd ed., vol. II, pt. 2, p.333.[a]
2. XIV, 6. [b]
3. "So when the physical power of certain climates violates the natural law..., it is for the legislator to make civil laws which overpower the nature of the climate and re-establish the original laws." (XVI, 12).
4. "The Japanese people have such an atrocious character that their legislators and magistrates have not been able to place any trust in them: they hold up to their view only judges, threats and chastisements." (XIV, 15).[c]

a normali statu deflectitur. Itaque politica scientia hac contingentia non evertitur ; sed tantum minuitur. Nempe pro materia solas fere habet normales politicae vitae formas. Morbi autem, nostri sententia, extra scientiam paene sunt, quia extra naturae leges ponuntur.

Ipsa autem naturalis legis conceptio, quam omnia haec continent, multum adhuc retinuit quod obscurum et incertum est. Leges enim sunt necessariae rerum connexiones ; si verbo interdum violari possunt, non veram necessitatem habent, sed mere logicam. Scilicet exprimunt quod in societatis definitione implicatur; societas autem aliam formam affectare potest quam quae ex sua natura rationaliter sequitur. Per eas igitur discimus non quod est, sed quod est rationale. Immo, quamvis Secundatus non existimet homines semper aut plerumque a recta via aberrasse, sed contra quod longa et generali experientia confirmatum est sponte revereatur, tamen quasdam deformitates omnibus ejusdem generis individuis esse confidit. Non sensit nihil fere in tota specie universale esse posse quod non certis necessitatibus respondeat. Exempli gratia, quamvis servitutis institutio apud omnes graecas italicasque antiquitatis civitates in usu fuerit, eam tamen a Reipublicae natura abhorrere declarat.[1] Quanquam jus repudii tantummodo virorum est ubicumque feminae in domestica servitute vivunt, in iisdem societatibus solis feminis hanc facultatem vindicat.[2] Quin est unum societatum genus, Tyrannis scilicet, quod Secundatus aliquid vitiosi et corrupti per se habere censet, quamvis idem in quibusdam locis necessarium esse ipse agnoscat.[3] Ordo

---

1. XV, 1, in fine.

2. XVI, 15.

3. « Le principe du gouvernment despotique se corrompt sans cesse, parce qu'il est corrompu par sa nature » (VIII, 10.)

from the normal state. So political science is not destroyed by this contingency. It is merely limited by it. Its concern is almost wholly with normal forms of political life. For Montesquieu, disease is more or less outside the scope of science, because it lies outside the laws of nature.

But the idea of natural law which all this involves is itself still quite vague and obscure. Laws are necessary connexions between things. Yet if they can sometimes be broken, they have a necessity which is purely logical rather than real. That is, they express what is implied in the definition of a society – although a society can take on a form other than that which follows rationally from its nature. They therefore tell us, not what exists, but what is rational. It is true that Montesquieu does not think that all or most of the time humanity errs and loses its way. He has an intuitive respect, instead, for what has the support of long, general experience. It is nonetheless his belief that there are some things which are pathological and yet characteristic of all members of the same type. He fails to realize that whatever is more or less universal in a type must correspond to definite necessities. For example, although the institution of slavery existed in all the ancient Greek and Italian city-states, he declares it contrary to the nature of a republic.[1] Although, wherever women live in domestic servitude, only men have the right to repudiate a spouse, he argues that in such societies it should be a power only of women.[2] There is even a whole type of society – despotism – which Montesquieu sees as in some way defective and corrupt in itself, although he himself acknowledges that in some places it is necessary.[3]

---

1. XV, 1, conclusion.
2. XVI, 15.
3. "The principle of despotic government is endlessly corrupted because it is corrupt by its nature." (VIII, 10).

igitur, quem in iis conditionibus scientia indagari debet, non modo non is est qui semper et ubique existat, sed etiam evenire potest ut nunquam exstiterit. Itaque leges, quae eum referunt, idealem quamdam formam necessario habent ; nam rerum connexiones exprimunt non quales sunt, sed quales esse debent. Non rebus insunt, ut ceterae naturae leges, aut potius non res ipsae sunt quatenus sub certo quodam adspectu considerantur, sed eas ex alto quasi dominantur, quamvis suae auctoritati non semper nec necessario obtemperetur.

Ea via est qua Secundatus ad antiquam politicae scientiae conceptionem pro parte revertitur ; sed pro parte tantum. Sane huc et illuc in eo est ut naturae leges cum praeceptis, quae quid faciendum sit edicunt, confundat. Sed procul abest quin, priscorum philosophorum instar, naturam, qualis est, omittat ut aliam instituat. Nempe, quanquam nullum certum principium ea de re statuit, sponte tamen intellexit in raris tantum casibus aliquid universale esse posse quod non simul sanum et rationale sit. Itaque societatum species, ut vidimus, ex historia describere et explicare tentavit, easque tantum corrigere ausus est cum in iis aliquid reperiret quod cum eorumdem essentia, qualem ex rerum observatione concluserat, congruere non arbitrabatur. Sin igitur apud Secundatum legis naturalis notio non ad totam politicam vitam, certe ad majorem hujus partem sese extendit. Si dubii aliquid et vagi adhuc retinet ex antiqua artis et scientiae confusione, hoc interdum tantum manifestum apparet.

Thus the order to be investigated in such terms by science is not only not something which exists everywhere and at all times, but it might even turn out that it has never existed. The laws which reproduce it necessarily have an ideal form. They express connexions between things, not as they are, but as they ought to be. They do not lie within things, like all other laws of nature. Or rather they are not things themselves, under a particular, definite aspect. Instead, it is as if they rule them from on high, though there is not always, or necessarily, submission to their authority.

This is how Montesquieu reverts, in part, to the ancient conception of political science – but only in part. Of course, he is inclined at this or that point to confuse laws of nature with rules which bring out what should be done. But it is far from the case that he ignores, like earlier philosophers, nature as it is, to install another. Though he did not lay down any definite principle on the matter, he instinctively understood that, with rare exceptions, whatever is universal must at the same time be both sound and rational. As we have seen, he tried to describe and explain types of societies on the basis of history, and suggested reform only when he discovered something in them which he did not think compatible with their essential nature, as he had inferred it from observation of things. So with Montesquieu the idea of natural law extends, even if not to the whole of political life, at least to the greater part of it. If there is still a vagueness and uncertainty that it owes to the old confusion of art and science, this only occasionally becomes apparent.

CAPUT QUINTUM

DE METHODO QUAM SECUNDATUS SECUTUS
EST

I

Quamdiu Politica in arte consistebat, politici scriptores deductione praecipue utebantur. Scilicet ex universali hominis notione trahebant quae societatis forma humanae naturae conveniret et quae praecepta in communi vita observanda essent. Hujus methodi vitia inutile est enumerare. Per deductionem enim, in ipsa arte, nihil aliud assequi possumus quam meras hypotheses. Sola vi rationis nemo asserere potest praeceptum aliquod utile esse cujus utilitatem non expertus sit. Sed in scientia, praesertim cum ab arte separatur, necesse est deductio secundas tantummodo partes occupet, certe ubi de rebus, non de abstractis notionibus, ut in mathematicis, agitur. Sane deductio cogitationes nobis suppetit quae nostram investigationem per rerum ambages ducunt ; sed quoad observatione confirmatae sunt, incertum est num res vere exprimant. Naturae leges nulla alia via reperiri possunt quam si natura ipsa attente consideretur. Immo observare non satis est, oportet praeterea ut eam interrogemus, sollicitemus, omni modo tentemus. Politicae igitur scientiae, propterea quod res pro materia habet, experimentalis methodus sola succedere potest.

Hanc autem methodum non facile est nostrae scientiae

CHAPTER FIVE

ON THE METHOD MONTESQUIEU FOLLOWED

I

As long as politics consisted in art, political writers mainly made use of deduction. They derived, from a universal idea of man, the form of society which suited human nature and the rules which ought to be observed in common life. Drawing up a list of the method's shortcomings is pointless. Even in art itself all we can arrive at, *via* deduction, are pure hypotheses. Nobody can establish, by the sheer force of reason, the value of a rule the value of which is untested by experience. But it is in science, especially once separated from art, that it is necessary that deduction has only a secondary role, at least when it is a matter, not as in mathematics of abstract concepts, but of realities. Of course, deduction comes to our help with ideas that steer research through the obscurity of things. But it is uncertain, until they are confirmed by observation, if they do in fact express things. There is no way in which laws of nature can be discovered without a careful study of nature itself. Indeed, it is not enough to observe it; it is necessary to go beyond this and interrogate it, turn it over and over and put it through every kind of test. Since political science deals with things, only the experimental method can succeed in it.

Yet the method is not easy to apply in our science,

accommodare, quia experimenta in societatibus tentari
nequeunt. Est tamen obliqua via qua difficultas
exsuperatur. Etenim ad naturae leges reperiendas nihil
aliud necessarium est quam satis multas comparationes
inter varias ejusdem rei formas institui posse. Hac enim
arte constantes immotaeque connexiones, quas lex
exprimit, a ceteris, id est fugitivis fortuitisque, secer-
nentur. Itaque tota experimentationis vis in eo tantum
consistit ut res fere ad libitum variet atque ita amplam
uberamque comparationi materiam praebeat. At nil obstat quin civilia ejusdem generis facta, qualia apud
varias societates occurrunt, comparemus atque note-
mus quae eorum ubique coeant, quae simul evanescant,
quae eodem tempore et secundum eamdem rationem
mutentur. Eae igitur comparationes, quanquam hoc incom-
modi habent ut non in infinitum renoventur, experimentationis tamen partes in politica scientia tenere
possunt.

Quanquam Secundatus hanc quaestionem nusquam
agitavit, tamen hujus methodi necessitatem sponte
sensit. Etenim nullo alio proposito tot facta ex variarum
gentium historia collegit nisi ut ea inter se conferret
illaque collatione eorumdem leges inveniret. Revera
manifestum est opus totum in legum comparatione
consistere quas diversissimi populi observant eoque
libro noster vere dici potest hoc novum studiorum
genus instaurasse quod hodierna nostra linguit *droit
comparé* appellamus.

At, si deductio apud Secundatum experientiae cessit,
multo majus spatium adhuc obtinet quam scientiae
natura patitur.

Ipse enim, jam in sua praefatione, legentem monet
se Politicam more quasi mathematico tractare voluisse ; id
est principia posuisse unde particulares societatum leges[a]

since there cannot be experiments with societies. However, there is an indirect way of overcoming the difficulty. All that is necessary for the discovery of laws of nature is to be able to establish a sufficient number of comparisons between different forms of the same thing. It is by this technique that the fixed, constant connexions which express a law can be separated out from others, namely, the chance and the transient. Thus the whole point of experiment consists simply in varying things more or less at will so as to obtain data which form a rich, extensive basis for comparison. But there is nothing to stop us from comparing social facts of the same kind, as they occur in different societies, and noting which of them exist together everywhere, disappear simultaneously or change at the same time and according to the same pattern. So despite the drawback that such comparisons cannot be repeated indefinitely they can take the place, in political science, of experiment.

Although Montesquieu never went into the matter, he realized, instinctively, the need for this method. His project, in assembling so many facts from the history of different peoples, could only have been to compare them with one another and to discover, through doing so, their laws. Indeed, it is obvious that the entire work consists in a comparison of the laws observed by the most diverse peoples and it can be truly said that he inaugurated, with his book, the new discipline nowadays called *comparative law*.

But if, with Montesquieu, deduction gave way to experience, it still has a much greater place than the nature of science permits.

He himself makes it clear to readers in the preface that he has set out to treat politics in an almost mathematical manner; that is, he has enunciated principles from which

logice sequerentur.[1] Sane necessarium intellexit haec principia e rerum observatione trahere ;[2] sed in iis totam scientiam quasi implicari credit, ita ut, ubi semel ad ea pervenerimus, sola deductione absolvi possit. Nec dubium est quin hac via et ratione procedere revera susceperit. Primum enim animadverte quomodo inductiva methodo utatur. Non incipit facta omnia, quae ad quaestionem attinet, colligere, referre, ut aequa mente examinari et perpendi possint ; sed plerumque mera deductione primum probat quod in animo habet. Monstrat scilicet hoc in natura aut, si id dicere velis, essentia societatis, vel hominis, vel commercii, vel religionis, uno verbo in rerum, de quibus agitur, definitione involvi ; posterius tantum facta quae hypothesin confirmare videntur, exponit.[3] Qui vero pro comperto habet sola experientia demonstrari posse quae sint rerum connexiones, non deductionem experientiae praeficit ; non principem locum argumentis assignat quae nihil fere ad demonstrandum valere censet quibusque diffidit, sed primum res observat ac postea tantum quod observatum est deductione interpretatur.

Ceterum, si ipsas nostri demonstrationes consideres, facile videbis totam vim earum in deductione consistere.

---

1. « J'ai posé les principes, et j'ai vu les cas particuliers s'y plier comme d'eux-mêmes, les histoires de toutes les nations n'en être que les suites. »

2. « Je n'ai point tiré mes principes de mes préjugés, mais de la nature des choses. » (*Ibid.*)

3. Innumera exempli citari possint quae per totum opus invenies. Sic postquam tria societatum genera definit, ex iisdem definitionibus eorumdem principia deducit. « *Il ne m'en faut pas davantage pour trouver leurs trois principes ; ils en dérivent naturellement.* » (III, 2.)[a] Tum ex iis principiis leges quae ad jus civile, ad poenas, ad feminarum conditionem spectant, trahit. Vide ipsos titulos capitum VI et VII *(Conséquences des principes des [divers] gouvernements par rapport à la simplicité des lois [civiles et] criminelles, la forme des jugements, etc., – [Conséquences des différents principes des trois gouvernments] par rapport aux lois somptuaires, etc.)*[b]

particular laws of society follow logically.[1] Of course, he understood the need to base such principles on empirical observation.[2] But in his view it is as if a science is wholly contained within these, and so can be completed just by deduction once we arrive at them. Nor is there any doubt that he in fact undertook to proceed along these lines. Let us notice, first, his use of the inductive method. He does not begin by collecting and reporting all the facts relevant to an enquiry, so that it is possible to examine and assess them objectively. He usually starts with a proof, by pure deduction, of what it is he has in mind. He shows that this is inherent in the nature or, it could be said, the essence of society, or of man, commerce, religion – in short, in the definition of the things in question. It is only later on that he sets out facts which seem to confirm the hypothesis.[3] If really sure that the connexions that exist between things can be shown only from experience, we do not set deduction above it. We do not give first place to arguments we suspect and consider almost worthless to try and demonstrate. We observe things first, and only afterwards interpret, by deduction, what has been observed.

Moreover, if we examine Montesquieu's proofs, it is easy to see that their whole force lies in deduction. True,

---

1. "I have set down the principles and have seen particular cases submit to them as though by themselves; the histories of all nations being merely the consequences."

2. "I did not draw my principles from my prejudices, but from the nature of things" (*ibid.*)

3. Innumerable examples can be given, to be found throughout the whole work. Thus after he defines the three types of societies, he deduces their principles from their definitions: "*Nothing more is needed for me to discover the three principles; they derive naturally from this*" (III,2).[a] He then infers from the principles the laws which concern civil law, punishment, the condition of women – as indicated by the very titles of Books VI and VII (*Consequences of the principles of the [various] governments in relation to the simplicity of [civil and] criminal laws, the form of judgments,* etc., and *in relation to sumptuary laws,* etc.).[b]

Sane quae ita concludit observatione plerumque confirmat ; sed quam infirma est tota haec argumentationis pars ! Facta quae ex historia refert breviter ac summatim exponit neque multum curat ut ea, qualia vere sunt, constituantur, etiamsi controversiae materiam praebeant.[1] Eadem praeterea sine ordine et confuse enumerat. Si causalem nexum inter duo facta esse asserit, non ea in omnibus aut saltem plerisque casibus simul apparere, vel simul deficere, vel eodem modo variari ostendit. Satis habet si exempla aliquot proferri possunt quae cum lege supposita non male quadrent. Immo evenit ut de tota specie aliquid affirmet quod apud unam societatem observavit. Sic magistratuum divisionem, quanquam apud solos Anglos reperitur Monarchiae propriam esse dicit[2] et ex ea divisione libertatem sequi declarat quanquam inscius est num apud ipsos Anglos vere exstiterit.[3] Uno verbo, non deductione utitur ut quod experientia probatum est interpretetur, sed potius experientia ut deductionis conclusiones exemplis explanet. Ergo, cum deductio peracta est, fere tota demonstratio perfecta esse ei videtur.

Quin etiam sunt, Secundati sententia, ut jam diximus, quaedam instituta quae, quamvis in omnibus ejusdem generis societatibus exstent aut exstiterint, iisdem tamen non conveniunt. Hoc autem unam ob rationem affirmat et affirmare potest : scilicet quia haec instituta

---

1. Sic quae de frugalitate et aequalitate apud antiquos, aut de causis quae societatum principia corrumpunt, aut de feminarum conditione dicit (XVI). Omnia haec innumeras quaestiones et difficultates involvunt quae non statim solvi possunt.

2. XI, 6.

3. « Ce n'est point à moi à examiner si les Anglais jouissent actuellement de cette liberté, ou non. Il me suffit de dire qu'elle est établie par leurs lois. » (XI, 6.)

he usually backs up the conclusions that he reaches in this way with observation. Yet how weak is this entire part of his argument! He reports historical facts in a brief, summary fashion, with little effort to establish their truth, even though they are the subject of controversy.[1] And he sets them down without order and method. If he claims there is a causal link between two facts, he does not demonstrate that in all or at least most cases they show up at the same time, or disappear at the same time, or vary in the same way. He is satisfied if a number of examples can be given which do not square that badly with the supposed law. Indeed, it turns out that he asserts, as true of a type, something he has observed just in a single society. Thus although the division of powers is found only amongst the English he says that it is an essential characteristic of monarchy,[2] and insists that freedom follows from this division but without knowing if it really exists amongst the English themselves.[3] In sum, instead of using deduction to interpret what has been proved by experience he uses experience to explain, with examples, the conclusions of deduction. Once a deduction has been made, almost all of a proof seems to him complete.

It is even the case in Montesquieu's view, as earlier pointed out, that there are certain institutions which exist or have existed in all societies of the same type and yet which do not fit in with them. It is something he asserts and is able to assert for just one reason, namely, that he does not

---

1. As in what he says on frugalness and equality amongst the ancients, or on the causes which corrupt the principles of societies, or on the condition of women (XVI). These all involve innumerable questions and difficulties which cannot be cleared up straightaway.

2. XI, 6.

3. "It is not my task to examine whether or not the English actually do have this freedom. It is enough for me to say that it is instituted in their laws." (XI, 6).

e principiis, quae antea posuit, non deduci posse existimat. Etenim servitutis institutionem et Reipublicae definitionem inter se contraria esse ostendit. Sic Tyrannida odit quia societatis atque etiam hominis essentiae, qualem esse concipit, logice repugnat.[1] Deductio igitur in quibusdam casibus etiam contra observationem et experientiam praevalet.

Sin ergo inductio in politica scientia primum apud Secundatum apparet, contraria methodo nondum discessit eaque admixtione adulteratur. Ut noster novam viam ingressus est, ita tamen tritam non deseruit. Ea autem methodi ambiguitas ex ipsa doctrinae, quam supra retulimus, ambiguitate sequitur. Etenim si normales societatis formae in ejusdem natura comprehenduntur, ex hujus naturae definitione concludi possunt; eas autem logicas necessitudines Secundatus leges appellat. Si res adeo rationi nostrae cognatae sunt, ratio sufficit ad eas interpretendas. Miraberis forsitan hanc intimam rerum naturam adeo apertam videri ut jam e scientiae exordio cognosci et definiri possit, cum contra scientia peracta potius quam incipiente determinari posse videatur. Hoc autem cum Secundati principiis bene constat. Quemadmodum vinculum, quod inter politica facta et societatis essentiam existit, rationabile est, ita et ea ipsa essentia, quae totius hujus deductionis fons est, eamdem naturam habet, id est in simplici notione consistit quam ratio celeri inspectione amplecti valet. Uno verbo, Secundatus non satis sentit quantum, ut ait Verulamius, rerum subtilitas humanae mentis subtilitatem exsuperet :[a] ea est causa cur rationi et

---

1. « Après tout ce que nous venons de dire, il semblerait que la nature humaine se soulèverait [sans cesse] contre le gouvernement despotique. » (V, 14.)

think it possible to deduce these institutions from the principles he has already laid down. He shows that the institution of slavery conflicts with the definition of a republic, and condemns despotism as logically incompatible with the essence of society and indeed of man as he conceives it.[1] Thus there are cases in which deduction prevails even in the face of observation and experience.

If, then, induction makes its first appearance in political science with Montesquieu, it has still not broken away from the opposite method and is corrupted by the connexion. In setting out on a new route he did not quit old ground. This ambiguity in method follows from the ambiguity in doctrine already discussed. If a society's normal forms are contained in its nature, they can be inferred from a definition of this nature; it is these logical necessities that Montesquieu calls laws. If things are as closely tied up with our reason, reason is enough for an understanding of them. It is perhaps surprising that this inner nature of things appears so accessible that it can be recognized and defined right from the start of a science, when it is in an established rather than emergent science that its determination seems possible. But this very much fits in with Montesquieu's principles. Just as the connexion which exists between political facts and a society's essence is rational, so this essence – the source of the entire deduction – has the same nature, consisting in a simple notion reason can quickly get hold of. In sum, Montesquieu does not sufficiently appreciate how much, in Bacon's words, the subtlety of things surpasses the subtlety of the human mind;[a]

---

1. "After everything we have said, it may seem that human nature should [constantly] rise up against despotic government." (V, 14).

deductioni adeo confidat. Ceterum non contendimus res civiles per se absurdas esse. Sed si quaedam logica in iis latet, alia est atque illa quam in deducendo observamus ; non eamdem simplicitatem habet ; quin alias leges forte sequitur. Itaque necesse est eam e rebus ipsis ediscamus.

Haec autem confusio ab alia causa quoque pendet. Societatis leges, ut vidimus, violari possunt ; ergo ex sola rerum observatione atque etiam comparatione constitui nequeunt. Quod est, non necessario rationale est ; leges autem nihil habent quod non rationale sit. Itaque etiamsi aliquid historia comprobaveris, non omnino certus eris id verum esse. Sunt vitia quae apud omnes ejusdem generis gentes occurrunt. Ergo ex eo quod apud istas reperitur earumdem normalis forma describi non potest. Si rerum natura experientia non fideliter deprehenditur, non ex sola experientia disces quae ex natura sequuntur. Nulla igitur alia via restat quam ut hanc ipsam essentiam assequamur, definiamus atque ex ea definitione id quod involvit deducamus. Ne concludas autem observationem ideo inutilem, sed aliquatenus suspectam habendam esse quamdiu deductione non confirmata est, et, si, forte confirmari non possit, rejiciendam. Vides quam necessarium sit in politica scientia signum certum in rebus ipsis invenire quo morbus et bona valetudo secernantur. Eo enim deficiente, ad deductionem necessario confugitur et simul a rebus receditur.

II

Sive autem deductione seu inductione procedat, regulam quamdam methodi sequitur quae praesenti scientiae retinenda est.

hence his confidence in reason and deduction. Yet it is not our claim that social things are in themselves irrational. But if a certain logic lies hidden in them, it is different from the one we use in deductive reasoning; it does not have the same simplicity; perhaps it even follows other laws. Thus we need to find out about it from things themselves.

However, this confusion also has another cause. The laws of society, as we have seen, can be broken. Therefore they cannot be established just by observation and indeed comparison of things. The actual is not necessarily the rational; but laws do not consist of anything which is not rational. So even if we demonstrate something from history we cannot be completely certain it is true. There are pathologies which occur amongst all peoples of the same type. Therefore their normal form cannot be described from what is found amongst them. If the nature of things cannot be discovered faithfully from experience, we cannot learn just from experience what follows from this nature. So the only course left to us is to grasp this essence, define it and deduce from the definition what it involves. Then the point is not that observation is useless, but that it is to some extent to be held suspect as long as it is not confirmed by deduction, and, if it turns out it cannot be so confirmed, to be rejected. It can be seen how necessary it is in political science to find in things themselves a reliable sign by which to distinguish health and malaise. Without this, it is inevitably forced to resort to deduction and, at the same time, to retreat from things.

II

But whether he proceeds by deduction or induction, he follows a rule of method that it is necessary for modern science to retain.

Res politicae per diversas species vulgo dividuntur quas, prima quidem inspectione, nullam inter se cognationem habere dicas. Est enim alia religionis natura, alia juris et morum, alia commercii aut administrationis. Itaque de unaquaque classe separatim tractari diu solitum est atque etiam nunc solet, quasi per se, abstractisque aliis, explorari et explicari possit, haud secus atque in physica de corporum gravitate, seorsus a colore, disseritur. Ceterum eamdem factorum classem cum aliis communicare non ideo negatur, sed leviter tantum, ita ut, cum intima rerum natura non attingatur, omnia haec commercia sine incommodo negligi possint. Sic, exempli gratia, plerique qui de ethica scribunt, mores et vivendi praecepta, quae in usu sunt aut esse debent, tractant quasi per se existentia, neque ab iis curatur quae sit apud easdem societates divitiarum natura ; qui vero de divitiis, non minore vehementia contendunt scientiam quam colunt, politicam oeconomiam scilicet, omnino sui juris esse, suoque munere fungi posse etiamsi hoc regularum corpus, quod ethicam constituit, prorsus ignoretur. Multa alia ejusdem generis exempla referri possint.

Secundatus contra bene perspexit omnia haec inter se ita cohaerere ut singula per se, remotis ceteris, intelligi nequeant ; itaque non jus a moribus, a religione, a commercio, etc., separat neque praesertim a societatis forma quae suam vim ad omnes res civiles extendit. Etenim, quamvis diversa sint, unius ejusdemque societatis vitam exprimunt ; variis ejusdem corporis politici partibus aut organis respondent. Sin autem non quaeratur quomodo organa inter se consentiant aliaque ab aliis afficiantur, quale sit uniuscujusque munus definiri non poterit. Immo eorumdem natura prorsus latebit : nam totidem res per se existentes esse videbuntur,

It is common to distinguish different sorts of political matters and affairs that, it may be said, are not in any obvious way related. The nature of religion is one thing, of law and morals another, as is that of commerce, or of administration. So for a long time it was usual, and still is even today, to treat each class separately, as if they can be investigated and explained by themselves, abstracting out others, and just as weight is studied in physics without reference to colour. This is not to claim that a class of facts does not have any links with others. But it is in so unimportant a way that the essential nature of things is unaffected and all these relationships can be safely ignored. For example, most writers on ethics treat morals and the rules that are or ought to be followed in the conduct of life as if these exist on their own, and are uninterested in the nature of wealth in the societies concerned – while writers on wealth are no less insistent that their science, political economy, is fully autonomous and can carry out its task even though not taking any notice of the body of rules that constitutes ethics. And it is possible to give many other examples of this kind.

Montesquieu, in contrast, realized that all these things are so interconnected that they cannot be understood, each just on its own, divorced from the others. Thus he does not set law apart from morality, religion, commerce, etc., or, above all, from the form of society which spreads and extends its influence to everything in the social world. However diverse they may be, they express the life of one and the same society. They correspond with different parts or organs of the same political system. Unless there is investigation into the ways in which they harmonize and are affected by one another, the function that each has cannot be determined. Indeed, their nature will remain completely hidden. They will be seen as so many separately

dum rei partes tantummodo sunt. Inde nati sunt errores qui apud multos etiam nunc valent. Inde fit enim ut politica oeconomia privatae utilitatis curam unicum societatis principium saepissime habuerit et legislatori jus denegaverit in negotiis quae ad commercium et operosas artes attinent sese immiscendi. Contra, sed ob eamdem causam, in ethica jus dominii tanquam aliquid per se immotum et inconcussum plerumque habetur, dum e conditionibus pendet quas divitiarum scientia determinat quaeque maxime instabiles et diversae sunt.

Immo vero hunc errorem discutere necessarium erat non modo ut politica scientia proficeret, sed etiam constitueretur. Sane diversa illa studia, quae sub variis titulis de politicis rebus separatim tractabant, illam praeparavere quippe quae ex iis constet. Attamen vere tantum exstitit cum manifestum tandem apparuit particulares illas scientias arcta necessitudine inter se conjungi et membra unius corporis esse. Ad eam autem animi conceptionem perveniri non poterat quamdiu ignorabatur omnia quae in societate fiunt inter se cognata esse. Secundatus ergo, mutuas politicarum rerum connexiones demonstrando, hanc unitatem scientiae nostrae praesentit, confuse quidem. Etenim nusquam dicit his quaestionibus, quas agitat, definitam quamdam scientiam constitui posse quae omnia civilia facta amplectatur, quae suam methodum habeat proprioque nomine appellanda sit. Sed, in re, primum hujus scientiae specimen quasi inscius posteritati dedit. Sin igitur quod in suis principiis involvebatur, non expresse concludit, certis successoribus suis viam aperuit qui, cum *sociologiam* instituent, fere nihil aliud novi facient nisi studiorum generi, quod noster tentavit, nomen imponent.

existing realities, when they are merely parts of a reality. This is the source of errors which are still widely current. It is why political economy has so often erected concern with self-interest into the sole principle of society and denied the legislator the right to intervene in commercial and industrial matters. In contrast, but for the same reason, the right of ownership is usually viewed in moral philosophy as if it is something fixed and permanent in itself, when it depends on conditions determined by the science of wealth and which are highly unstable and diverse.

It was necessary to dispel this error, not only for political science to develop and progress, but to come into being in the first place. No doubt the different, separate, variously named studies of political subjects prepared the way for it, in that it is, of course, made up of them. Yet it did not truly exist until it at last became clear that these particular sciences are linked together by a strict necessity and are parts of a whole. But it was impossible to arrive at this view as long as it was not realized that everything in society is connected up with everything else. In showing such interrelationships, Montesquieu looked ahead to the unity of our science, although in a vague and confused way. He never says that the enquiries which preoccupy him can form the basis of a definite science which covers all social facts, which has its own method, and which needs to have its own name. In fact, however, he provided those who came after him with the first, although not explicit, example of this science. So even if he did not clearly set out the conclusions which are implied by his principles, he opened the way to his successors who, in inaugurating *sociology*, did not do much more than bestow, on the kind of study undertaken by him, a name.

III

Est autem peculiaris quaedam notio quae, temporibus nostris, politicae scientiae methodum renovavit quamque Secundatus ignorasse videtur ; haec est — si Gallicum verbum in latinam linguam paene integrum transferre liceat — notio progressus. Sed in quo illa consistat videamus.

Si populi inter se comparantur, primum apparet certas formas aut proprietates, quae intimae societatum naturae manifeste inhaerent, apud quosdam vix inchoatas, apud alios contra insigniores esse ; alii parvi sunt et per vasta spatia dispersi, alii majores et densi ; alii omni stabilito imperio carent, dum apud alios reipublicae administratio non modo constituitur, sed ad omnes corporis politici partes suam vim extendit ; atque sunt inter eos innumeri gradus interpositi. Itaque, quod ad hoc pertinet, non omnes, ut ita dicam, dignitatem habent, sed alii aliis superiores aut inferiores dici possunt. Praeterea observatum est superiores ex inferioribus natos esse. Equidem non dico societatum seriem rectae lineae formam habere cujus novissimi populi summam, antiqui vero imam extremitatem occupent ; contra arboris speciem potius affectat cujus rami in diversas regiones extenduntur. At parum id propositi refert. Nihilominus verum restat societates alias ab aliis ortas esse et recentiores prioribus praestare ; hoc est quod humani generis progressionem appellamus. Si vero unum populum ex se consideres, idem reperietur. Scilicet ex tempore quo esse incipit supra speciem, e qua ortus est, sese paulatim extollit humanaeque naturae progressus

III

But there is a particular idea that has transformed the method of political science in our time and that Montesquieu does not seem to have known about. This – if a French term may be reproduced, more or less as it stands, in Latin – is the idea of progress. Let us see what it involves.

If peoples are compared with one another, it is at once apparent that certain forms or properties clearly tied up with the essential nature of societies are hardly developed amongst some, but much more highly so amongst others. Some are small and scattered across vast territories, others are larger and heavily concentrated; some lack any established authority, while amongst others not only is there a state but its power extends throughout the political system; and there are innumerable intermediate forms between these. So, as far as this is concerned, they are not all of the same rank, but some can be said to be superior, others inferior. And it has been observed that the superior originate in the inferior. I am certainly not saying that the evolution of societies forms a single straight line, with modern peoples at the top and the ancient at the bottom; it is more like a tree, with branches spreading in different directions. But this has little to do with the point. It remains the case that societies arise out of one another and the more recent overtake and surpass those that came earlier; this is what we term human progress. The same is found in studying a particular people. From the time it first comes into existence it gradually raises itself above the type in which it had its origins, and the progress of human nature

e singulis illis incrementis, quae sensim accumulata sunt, constat.

Haec autem Secundatus non perspexit. Sane non omnes societates in aequo ponit ; Rempublicam et Monarchiam Tyrannidi[1] praefert, Reipublicae Monarchiam,[2] Rempublicam vero barbarorum democratiae.[3] At non suspicatur varias illas societatum species ex eadem stirpe descendisse aliasque aliis successisse ; contra singulas putat seorsum a ceteris constitutas esse. Monarchia quidem excipienda est quam ex inferiore democratia natam esse dicit.[4] Sed ex ea ipsa exceptione melius etiam patet quam longe ab ea progressus notione Secondatus absit ; nempe, hoc societatum genus, quod non nullo alio superius[a] esse censet, ex eo quod omnium infimum habetur protinus natum existimat. Ob eamdem rationem, cum de singulis gentibus loquitur, earum sane principium crescere posse aut corrumpi non negat,[5] sed idem fixum et definitum ex primo initio esse credit atque integrum per totam earum historiam servandum esse.[6] Non sentit societatum naturam contraria, quae inter se certant, in se habere propterea quod ex antecedenti forma paulatim tantum sese exsolvit paulatimque ad eam tendit quae

---

1. « L'inconvénient n'est pas lorsque l'État passe d'un gouvernment modéré [à un gouvernement modéré], comme de la république à la monarchie, ou de la monarchie à la république, mais quand il tombe et se précipite du gouvernment modéré au despotisme. » (VIII, 8.)

2. XI, 8, in fine.

3. « Comme les peuples qui vivent sous une bonne police sont plus heureux que ceux qui, sans règle et sans chefs, errent dans les forêts. » (V, 11.)

4. Monarchiam germanorum gentium corruptione exstitisse dicit (XI, 8), germanos autem barbarorum vitam duxisse (XVIII, 22 et 30. Cf. XVIII, 14.)

5. « Un État peut changer de deux manières : ou parce que la constitution se corrige, ou parce qu'elle se corrompt. » (XI, 13.)

6. « S'il (l'État) a conservé ses principes, et que la constitution change, c'est qu'elle se corrige : s'il a perdu ses principes, quand la constitution vient à changer, c'est qu'elle se corrompt. » (XI, 13.) [b]

consists in these particular, slowly accumulating developments.

Montesquieu did not see this. Of course he does not place all societies on the same level. He prefers the republic and monarchy to despotism,[1] monarchy to the republic,[2] and the republic to primitive democracy.[3] But he does not suspect that these different sorts of society descended from the same roots and succeeded one another. He believes they were each formed separately from the others. Monarchy is an exception – he says it arose out of primitive democracy.[4] Yet this exception makes it even clearer how far Montesquieu is from the notion of progress. He thinks that the type of society regarded by him as superior[a] to any other arose immediately out of the one considered the most primitive of all. For the same reason, in discussing particular peoples, he does not deny that their principle can grow or be corrupted,[5] but believes this is fixed and definite from the very beginning and must remain intact throughout their entire history.[6] He does not realize that the nature of societies contains opposites, which struggle with one another, just because it frees itself from an earlier form only little by little and moves little by little

---

1. "The trouble is not when the state passes from moderate government [to moderate government], as from republic to monarchy or from monarchy to republic, but when it falls and collapses from moderate government into despotism." (VIII, 8).

2. XI, 8, conclusion.

3. "Just as peoples who live under a good system of police are happier than those who, without rule and without leaders, wander in the forests." (V, 11).

4. He says that monarchy appeared through the corruption of the German peoples (XI, 8), and that the Germans led the life of barbarians (XVIII, 22 and 30. *Cf.* XVIII, 14).

5. "A state can change in two ways: either because its constitution is corrected or because it is corrupted." (XI, 13).

6. "If it (the state) has preserved its principles and its constitution changes, the latter corrects itself: if it has lost its principles when its constitution starts to change, the constitution is corrupted." (XI, 13).[b]

e se ipsa nascetur. Eum latit perpetuus ille processus in quo societas, quamvis sibi ipsi semper constet, tamen novum aliquid continuo evadit.

Inde autem aliquid singulare in usurpata methodo secutum est.

Sunt enim duo conditionum genera quae politicam vitam movent. Aliae in praesentibus circumstantiis jacent, ut natura soli, civium numero, etc.; aliae in praeterita historia versantur. Etenim quemadmodum puer quivis alius esset si alios habuisset genitores, societas alia est secundum societatum antecedentium formam. Si inferioribus populis succedit, non idem esse potest atque si e perpolitis nationibus orta est. Secundatus autem, propterea quod hanc societatum successionem et cognationem ignorat, hujus generis causas omnino negligit. Eam vim quae populos, ut ita dicam, a tergo impellit minime curat et circumfusa tantum respicit. Cum alicujus societatis historiam interpretari suscipit, non quaerit quem locum in societatum serie teneat, sed tantum quale sit solum, quam multi sint cives, etc. Nihil igitur huic methodo magis contrarium est quam Comte recentius in iisdem quaestionibus tractandis secutus est. Comte enim societatum naturam ex temporis momento, quo apparuerunt, totam pendere existimat scientiamque politicam paene integram consistere in societatum serie constituenda. Addere autem supervacuum est utraque doctrina unam tantum veritatis partem exprimi.

to one born out of this. What lay hidden from him was the continuous process in which society, while always keeping to its own nature, forever embarks on an ascent of something new.

This accounts for the peculiarity of the method he took up and followed.

There are two kinds of conditions at work in political life. Some lie in present circumstances such as geography, population size, etc. Others are rooted in the past and what has already taken place in history. Just as any child would be different with different parents, a society varies according to the form of preceding societies. It cannot be the same if it develops out of primitive rather than civilized peoples. As a result of not understanding the succession and connectedness of societies, Montesquieu completely overlooks causes of this kind. He is not at all concerned with the force that drives societies "from behind" and pays attention only to their existing environment. When he undertakes an account of the history of a society, he does not ask about its place in the evolution of societies, but only about geography, population size, etc. Nothing is more opposed to the method Comte later adopted in tackling the same questions. In Comte's view the nature of societies is totally dependent on the moment of time at which they made their appearance and almost all of political science consists in establishing the evolutionary sequence of societies. It hardly needs to be added that each of the two approaches expresses only one side of the truth.

CONCLUSIO

In sua politicae philosophiae historia P. Janet, postquam Secundati doctrinam exposuit, merito queritur
quod plerique, qui de eo scripserunt, sibi tantum
proposuere singulos errores quos admiserit persequi,
additque multo melius et aequabilius futurum esse si
quis accurate demonstret quam ampla et obscura
materia esset quam noster suscepit, et quanta vi ingenii
ea potitus sit.[1] Hoc est quod tentavimus. Secundati
enim opiniones de singulis quaestionibus quae in ejus
libro agitantur, praeterivimus et in eo tantum consti-
timus quod praecipua ejus laus esse nobis videtur. Scilicet quanquam cujuslibet scientiae originem ab hoc aut
illo homine numerare semper falsi aliquid habet, — fit
enim omnis scientia e continuis incrementis neque
facile dici potest quo temporis puncto esse inceperit —
certum tamen est praecipua politicae scientiae principia
apud Secundatum primum constituta esse.[2] Non ea
quidem expressis verbis professus est ; nempe de
scientiae conditionibus quam instauravit non multum

---

1. *Histoire de la Science politique,* tertia editio, II, 397-399. [a]
2. Comte quidem in suo *Cours de philosophie positive* (IV,178-185)[b]
jam agnovit quantum Secundatus de politica scientia meritus sit. Hoc autem
judicium brevissimum est, pro parte falsum, ut supra vidimus, ac
praesertim non ex attenta ac diligenti doctrinae meditatione sequi videtur.

CONCLUSION

Paul Janet, in his history of political philosophy, rightly complains after setting out Montesquieu's theory that most commentators have just wanted to expose particular errors he made, and adds that it would have been much better as well as fairer to have built up a careful picture of the vastness and obscurity of the subject tackled by him, and of the intellectual force and ingenuity with which he mastered it.[1] This is what we have tried to do. We have set aside Montesquieu's views on particular issues discussed in his book, and have concentrated on what seems to us his outstanding achievement. Although there is always something mistaken in dating a science's origin from this or that individual – since every science comes about through continuous advances and developments, and it can be difficult to say at what point it has come into existence – it is unquestionably the case that the fundamental principles of political science were established, for the first time, by Montesquieu.[2] He did not, indeed, set them out explicitly; he did not theorize much about the conditions of the science

---

1. *History of Political Science*, 3rd edition, II, 397-399. [a]

2. Comte already acknowledged, in his *Course of Positive Philosophy* (IV, 178-85),[b] how much Montesquieu deserved recognition in political science. But it is a very brief judgment, that is in part mistaken, as already seen, and that above all does not seem based on attentive, careful reflection on the theory.

philosophatur. Sed in ipsa ejus doctrina latent nec difficile est ea perspicere et in lucem edere.

Qualia vero essent supra vidimus. Non modo intellexit res politicas scientiae materiam esse, sed cardinales, ut ita dicam, notiones, quae hujus scientiae institutioni necessariae erant, pro parte constituit. Eae autem duae sunt : notio generis ac notio legis.

Earum prior in Secundati libro sine dubio apparet. Monstrat enim non modo summi imperii constitutionem, sed totam civilem vitam e societatibus diversam esse, diversas vero illas formas eas tamen esse quae inter se conferri queant. Hoc autem necessarium erat ut genera ac species distinguerentur ; nam non satis est societates ex una aut altera parte quasdam similitudines offerre, sed totam earumdem structuram et vitam comparari posse oportet. Quin etiam, non modo principia posuit, sed iis haud infeliciter usus est ; ea enim divisio quam tentavit ipsam rerum divisionem non sine quadam veritate exprimit. Duobus punctis tantum peccat. Primum falso posuit formas societatum e summi imperii formis sequi iisque definiri posse. Praeterea unum ex generibus quae distinguit, id est Tyrannida, aliquid vitiosi per se habere ducit ; quod a generis natura abhorret. Nam unicuique generi sua perfectio est quae, pro temporis locique conditionibus quibus respondet, ceterorum perfectioni aequa est.

Legis vero notionem difficilius erat ex aliis scientiis, ubi jam existebat, in nostram transferre. Etenim in omni scientia generis notio prior semper apparet quia humana mente promptius concipitur. Nam satis est oculos in res conjicere ut quaedam similitudines et differentiae in iis animadvertantur. Definitae autem illae connexiones, quas leges appellamus, quia rerum naturae propiores sunt, intra latent ; velamentum quasi iis ob-

he inaugurated. But they are implicit in his approach and it is not difficult to ascertain them and bring them to light.

We have seen what they are. He not only understood that political things are the object of a science, but helped to form the key ideas necessary to establish this science. They are two: the idea of type and the idea of law.

The first of these is undoubtedly apparent in Montesquieu's book. He shows that it is not only the constitution of the supreme power but the whole of social life which varies across societies, and that these different forms can nonetheless be seen in relation to one another. This was necessary in order to distinguish types, since it is not enough if in this or that aspect societies present certain similarities; it must be possible to compare their whole life and structure. Moreover, he not only laid down principles, but showed considerable judgment in applying them; the division he attempted expresses, not without a certain truth, the division itself of things. He was mistaken on just two points. First, he was wrong in holding that forms of society follow from forms of government and can be defined by these. Next, there is his view of one of the types he distinguishes – despotism – as involving something inherently corrupt about it, and this is incompatible with the nature of a type. Each type has its own ideal form, equal, in relation to the conditions of time and place with which it corresponds, to the ideal form of the others.

It was more difficult to carry over the idea of law from other sciences, where it already existed, to our own. In every science the idea of type always appears first, since it is easier for the human mind to conceive of it. It is enough to cast an eye on things to notice certain similarities and differences between them. But the definite connexions which we call laws, being more closely bound up with the nature of things, lie hidden within this; it is as if a veil is

tenditur quod primum removendum est ut ipsae attingi et in lucem proferri possint. Praeterea, quod ad politicam scientiam peculiariter attinet, propriae quaedam difficultates erant quae e natura ipsius politicae vitae sequebantur. Adeo enim mobilis est, adeo varia et multiformis ut ad certas immotasque leges redigi posse non videatur.[a] Adde quod homines non libenter credunt se eadem necessitate teneri atque ceteras res naturae.

Secundatus tamen, invita rerum specie, ordinem fixum et necessarium civilibus rebus inesse asserit ; societates negat ad libitum compositas esse[1] earumque historiam e fortuitis causis pendere ; sed pro comperto habet leges esse quae hanc mundi partem gubernent. Illas autem confuse concipit. Non exprimunt enim quomodo societatis natura civilia instituta gignat, sed quae sint instituta quae societatis natura requirit, quasi eorum causa efficiens in sola legislatoris voluntate quaerenda sit. Praeterea eo nomine Secundatus appellat notionum potius quam rerum connexiones. Sane eae sunt quas societas, si secum constet, necessario observet, sed sibi ipsi dissentiendi facultatem habet. Hujus tamen Politica non in meram dialecticam vertitur quia quod rationale est, id plerumque revera existere intellexit ; ea igitur idearum logica rebus quoque pro parte inest. Sunt vero exceptiones quae hujus notionis ambiguitatem produnt.

Ambiguitatem illam discutere, hoc est quod politica scientia post Secundatum ante omnia desiderabat. Etenim non longius progredi poterat quamdiu non demonstratum erat societatum leges non alias esse atque in reliqua natura neque methodum ad eas reperiendas

---

1. « J'ai d'abord examiné les hommes, et j'ai cru que, dans cette infinie diversité de lois et de moeurs, ils n'étaient pas uniquement conduits par leurs fantaisies. » (*Praef.*)

thrown over them, which first has to be taken off to be able to reach and reveal them. Moreover, where political science is particularly concerned, there were certain special difficulties, deriving from the very nature of political life. For it is so changeable, so diverse and multiform as not to seem[a] reducible to fixed and definite laws. Nor, it may be added, do men willingly believe that they are bound by the same necessity as other things in nature.

Montesquieu, however, asserts against appearances that there exists a fixed, necessary order in social things; he denies that societies have been constructed at will,[1] and that their history depends on chance causes; he is certain that there are laws which govern this part of the world. But his conception of them is confused. They do not express the way in which the nature of a society gives rise to social institutions, but what the institutions are which the nature of a society requires, as if their efficient cause is to be sought only in the will of the legislator. And Montesquieu describes as law connexions between ideas rather than between things. They are no doubt what a society, if faithful to its nature, necessarily observes, but it can go against them. However, his political theory is not turned into pure dialectic, since he grasped that what is rational is generally what exists in reality; thus his logic of ideas inheres, in part, also in things. There are, it is true, exceptions, which bring about the ambiguity in his notion.

It is the elimination of this ambiguity which political science, after Montesquieu, sought above all. It could not make further progress as long as it could not be shown that laws of societies are not different from others in the rest of nature and that the method for discovering them is not

---

1. "I began by examining men, and believed that, in the infinite diversity of laws and morals, they were not governed just by their fancy and imagination." (*Preface*).

aliam atque in ceteris naturae scientiis. Hoc est quod
Comte huic scientiae conferet. Ex legis notione alienum
illud, quod eam etiam tum vitiabat, purgabit atque
inductivae methodo, ut aequum est, primas partes vin-
dicabit. Tum scientia nostra conscia erit et quo tendere
debeat et qua via; tum omnia fere fundamenta, quae
necessaria erant ut aedificari posset, stabunt praepa-
rata. Ex hoc opusculo judicare licet quae pars in ea
praeparatione Secundati fuerit.[a]

different from the one in the other sciences of nature. It is here that Comte was to make his contribution. He eradicated from the concept of law the foreign elements which had vitiated it, and established the inductive method's rightful claim to primacy. Our science then knew both what to aim at and in what way; almost all the foundations necessary to develop it then stood prepared. It may be judged from this short study what the part was, in that preparation, of Montesquieu.[a]

SUR L'ŒUVRE DE TAINE[a]

Ce qui me paraît constituer l'œuvre propre de Taine, c'est qu'il a contribué plus que personne à introduire et à vulgariser en France une tradition philosophique qui, avant lui, ne comptait parmi nous que bien peu de représentants : c'est ce qu'on pourrait appeler l'empirisme rationaliste.

D'après l'empirisme, les choses ne sont pas intelligibles. Il n'y a pas entre elles de liens internes qui permettent de penser les unes à l'aide et en fonction des autres. Chaque fait particulier est comme étranger à ceux qui le précèdent comme à ceux qui le suivent et tout ce que l'esprit peut faire, c'est d'apercevoir et de retenir l'ordre extérieur dans lequel ils se succèdent le plus généralement. L'œuvre de la science consiste exclusivement à enregistrer le passé et à trouver des procédés mnemoniques qui permettent d'en garder plus facilement le souvenir. Tel est le rôle des idées générales, et des relations générales, purs artifices destinés à soulager la mémoire. L'esprit plierait sous le poids des connaissances infinies que suppose un monde infiniment divers si, par des simplifications méthodiques, il ne laissait de côté le détail pour s'en tenir aux aspects les plus généraux. Mais les schèmes qu'il construit ainsi ne correspondent à rien dans le réel; ils ne peuvent même pas être pensés en tant que tels, mais seulement à l'aide des mots. Ils ne sont l'objet que d'une intelligence verbale.

La thèse des rationalistes est exactement l'opposée de la précédente. D'après eux, il y a entre les choses des relations logiques, des rapports de parenté que la science a pour fin de découvrir et cette logique des choses est identique à celle de l'esprit. Aussi l'esprit, en la découvrant, ne fait-il que se retrouver lui-même; il a en lui les principes de toute intelligibilité.

ON THE WORK OF TAINE[a]

What seems to me to make Taine's work distinctively his own is that, more than anyone, he helped to introduce and popularize in France a philosophical tradition almost wholly unrepresented amongst us before him. It could be called "rationalist empiricism".

According to empiricism, things are not intelligible. There are no internal connexions between them, such that they may be thought in terms of and in relation to one another. Each particular fact is as separate from those preceding as from those following it, and all that the mind can do is to notice and hold on to the external order in which they most generally succeed one another. The work of science consists exclusively in recording the past and in finding mnemonic procedures that may make remembering it easier. Such is the role of general ideas and general relations, pure devices and props for the memory. The mind would collapse under the weight of an infinite knowledge supposed by an infinitely diverse world if it did not, through methodical simplification, set detail aside to stick to the most general appearances. But the schemas that it thus constructs do not correspond with anything in reality; they cannot even be grasped as such, but only through words. They are the object only of a verbal understanding.

The thesis of the rationalists is exactly the opposite. According to them, there are logical connexions between things, relations of affinity which it is the aim of science to discover and this logic of things is identical with that of the mind. Hence the mind, in discovering it, only rediscovers itself, and contains the principles of all intelligibility.

D'où il suit que non seulement le réel est intelligible, mais encore que cela seul est réel qui est pleinement intelligible, c'est-à-dire de même nature que l'entendement. Or, ce qui est le plus homogène à l'esprit, c'est l'élément simple et général. L'idée générale, le concept, au lieu d'être regardé comme une simple construction, commode mais arbitraire, devient ainsi le fond même de l'être. Le monde n'est qu'un système de concepts logiquement liés. Mais alors, qu'est-ce que le particulier, le complexe ? En vertu de ses principes, l'École est obligée de lui dénier plus ou moins complètement toute réalité. Elle y voit et ne peut y voir qu'une apparence trompeuse, un non-être, un voile jeté sur le fond intelligible des choses et qu'il faut écarter. Entre la sensation, où est donné le concret, l'individuel, et l'idée, qui exprime le général, il y a une solution de continuité. La première n'est pas le germe de la seconde ; ce n'est pas un premier stade de la connaissance qui prépare les autres ; c'est le stade de l'erreur qu'il ne faut traverser que pour s'en affranchir. De là l'éloignement de ces penseurs pour le sensible, le fait particulier, et la médiocre estime où ils tiennent les procédés qui, seuls, permettent de l'atteindre : l'observation et l'expérimentation. Puisque le monde est une pensé, la pensée, par ses seules forces, doit pouvoir le reconstruire.

Taine occupe une situation intermédiaire entre ces deux extrêmes. Avec les rationalistes, il admet qu'il existe entre les phénomènes des relations logiques, que les choses sont intelligibles. Quoiqu'on l'ait souvent considéré comme un pur disciple des Anglais, il reproche vivement à Mill d'avoir voulu réduire la science à n'être qu'une constatation des faits. Elle n'est complète que quand elle en rend compte, c'est-à-dire quand elle les déduit les uns des autres. Les rapports qu'elle pose, s'ils sont objectifs, sont nécessaires ; c'est-à-dire que les termes dont ils sont

It follows from this, not just that the real is intelligible, but that that alone is real which is fully intelligible, that is, of the same nature as the understanding. And it is the general, simple element which has most identity with mind. The general idea, the concept, instead of being seen as a mere construction, convenient but arbitrary, thus becomes the very foundation of being. The world is only a system of logically connected concepts. What about the particular, the complex? In virtue of its principles the school is forced to deny, more or less completely, all reality to this. It sees and can see in it only a deceptive appearance, a non-being, a veil thrown over the intelligible foundation of things which must be thrown off. There is a basic discontinuity between sensation, where there is the given of the individual and concrete, and the idea, which expresses the general. The first is not the germ of the second; it is not a first stage of knowledge preparing the way for others; it is the stage of error, necessary to cross only to free ourselves from it. Hence the disdain of these thinkers for the sensible, for the particular fact, and their low opinion of the procedures that alone allow getting at it – observation and experiment. Since the world is something thought, thought, just by its own powers, must be able to reconstruct it.

Taine occupies a middle position between these two extremes. He accepts, with the rationalists, that there exist logical connexions between phenomena, that things are intelligible. Although often considered a diehard disciple of the English, he very much criticizes Mill for having wanted to reduce science to a mere statement of facts. It is complete only when it gives an account of them, that is, when it derives them from one another. The relations which it sets out are, if objective, necessary; that is, the terms in which they are formed logically imply one

formés s'impliquent logiquement, et la raison peut trouver le pourquoi de cette implication. Mais, en même temps, il a un sentiment très vif de la réalité du fait, du phénomène concret, de l'être individuel. Le sensible, avec son infinie diversité, n'est pas pour lui une apparence ; c'est le réel, tout le réel.

Il a conscience de l'écart qu'il y a entre le simplisme naturel à l'entendement et l'énorme complexité des choses, et il en conclut que des opérations purement mentales ne sauraient suffire à nous en faire pénétrer la nature. Si nous voulons les comprendre, il nous faut sortir de nous-mêmes, nous mettre à leur école, apprendre d'elles ce qu'elles sont, c'est-à-dire recourir à l'observation et à l'expérimentation. Par là, il se rattache à l'empirisme. Nul n'a plus que lui le goût et même le culte du fait. On nous a rapporté que ce qu'il admirait le plus dans *Les premiers principes* de M. Spencer, c'est la quantité de documents qui y sont accumulés ; il l'appelait le livre aux, cent mille faits. Seulement cette méthode externe n'était, pour lui, que la première phase de la science ; celle-ci ne s'achève qu' en expliquant.

Ce qui fait l'importance de cette conception, c'est qu'elle seule permet d'assigner à la science sa véritable place.

Les empiristes, il est vrai, se sont généralement présentés comme les protagonistes de la science positive et leurs adversaires leur ont trop souvent laissé l'honneur et le bénéfice de ce rôle. En fait, comme ils ne séparent pas l'idée de la sensation, comme ils ne distinguent pas le sensible de l'intelligible, ils considèrent le monde tout entier comme soumis aux mêmes procédés d'investigation ; les méthodes qui ont réussi dans l'étude du monde matériel sont aussi celles qui doivent être employées à connaitre l'esprit, car il n'en existe pas d'autres. Mais ils n'aggrand-issent ainsi le champ de la connaissance scientifique qu'en

another, and reason can find the why and wherefore of this implication. At the same time, however, he has a very strong feeling for the reality of the fact, of the concrete phenomenon, of the individual being. The sensible, with its infinite diversity, is not for him an appearance; it is the real, all the real.

He is conscious of the gap between the *simplisme* natural to the understanding and the enormous complexity of things, and concludes that no purely mental operation can be enough to let us see and reach into their nature. If we want to understand them we must reach out of ourselves, go to their school and learn from them what they are – that is, turn to observation and experiment. He comes back, in this way, to a commitment to empiricism. Nobody had more taste for, indeed devotion to, the facts than he did. We are told that what he most admired about Spencer's *First Principles* was the quantity of documents amassed in it; he called it the book of a hundred thousand facts. It is just that for him this external method was no more than the first phase of science, which came into its own only when involving explanation.

What gives this conception its importance is that it alone is in a position to assign science its true and rightful place.

The empiricists, it is true, are generally hailed as the champions of positive science and their opponents have too often left them with the honour and credit of this role. In fact, since they do not separate sensation from idea, since they do not distinguish the sensible from the intelligible, they consider the world wholly and completely subject to the same procedures of investigation. The methods which have succeeded in the study of the material world are also those which must be employed for knowledge of the mind, because no others exist. But their

la rabaissant au niveau de la sensation ; car la science, telle qu'ils la conçoivent, est aveugle. Si elle s'étend à tout, elle n'éclaire rien. Sous couleur de positivisme, ils mettent partout le mystère. Suivant les rationalistes, au contraire, le mystère n'existe qu'à la surface et pour les sens ; tout l'effort de la réflexion doit tendre à le dissiper. Mais comme ils n'accordent au complexe qu'une demi-réalité, des moyens simples leur paraissent suffisants, pour arriver à leur but. Pour repenser le monde dans ce qu'il a d'explicable, c'est-à-dire et tant qu'il est semblable à l'esprit, c'est assez que l'esprit se replie sur lui-même et prenne conscience de sa nature. C'est de lui seul que peut venir la lumière. Une philosophie autonome, où le sujet s'exprime le plus adéquatement possible, sera la science véritable. Mais ces affirmations optimistes viennent se heurter à un sentiment très général et très fort et dont elles ne peuvent triompher : nous savons bien que les choses ne sont pas aussi claires, si transparentes, si faciles à pénétrer. Nous les sentons qui nous résistent au moment même où nous les pénétrons. L'humanité a trop conscience qu'il y a beaucoup de choses qu'elle ne comprend pas pour se tromper à ce point sur ses propres forces. Les progrès mêmes de la science ne peuvent que nous confirmer dans cette impression ; car ils sont infiniment lents et laborieux. Or il est inadmissible que, pour atteindre la surface de l'être, il faille tant de tours et de détours et que la route soit si courte pour aller au fond. Voilà pourquoi le rationalisme intempérant n'a jamais et ne peut avoir que des succès temporaires. Au moment précis où un peuple entreprend de se refaire un système d'idées, il peut bien, dans une crise d'enthousiasme et de confiance juvénile, croire que la tâche est aisée ; mais il ne tarde pas à en éprouver toutes les difficultés, et les illusions qu'il peut avoir eues ne font que rendre son désenchantement plus amer. L'empirisme ratio-

enlargement of the field of scientific knowledge merely reduces it to the level of sensation, since science, as they conceive it, is blind. If it extends to everything, it enlightens nothing. Under the guise of positivism they spread mystery everywhere. According to the rationalists, on the contrary, mystery exists only at the surface and for the senses. All effort of reflection must be about dispelling it. But because all they grant the complex is a half-reality, the ways that are sufficient to achieve their aim seem simple to them. To rethink the world in line with what is explicable in it – that is, as far as it is like the mind – it is enough for the mind to fall back on itself and be conscious of its nature. From it alone can come enlightenment. An autonomous philosophy, involving the subject's fullest possible self-expression, would be the true science. But these optimistic assertions run into very strong, very general sentiments which they cannot overcome. We know well enough that things are not so clear, so transparent, so easy to penetrate. We feel their resistance to us at the very moment of penetrating them. Mankind is too aware of the many things it does not understand to be deceived on this point about its own powers. The very advances of science can only confirm us in this impression, since they are extremely slow and laborious. It is inadmissible that, when the route to the mere surface of being is so tortuous, the route to its foundation is so short. This is why an intemperate rationalism never has, or can have, more than a temporary success. The particular moment at which a people sets out to change a system of ideas is a time when they can well believe, in an outburst of enthusiasm and youthful confidence, that the task is easy. But it does not take them long to experience all the difficulties, and the illusions they might have had only make their disenchantment more

naliste n'est exposé ni à l'un ni à l'autre de ces dangers. Tout en portant aussi loin que l'empirisme par le domaine de la science, tout en ouvrant le monde entier à la libre réflexion et en affirmant qu'il y a une explication possible des choses, il oppose une fin de non-recevoir aux explications sommaires et simples. Sans condamner la raison à abdiquer, sans même assigner de bornes à ses ambitions dans l'avenir, il la met en défiance contre elle-même. Il lui donne la sensation des ténèbres qui l'entourent, tout en lui reconnaissant le pouvoir d'y répandre peu à peu la clarté. Il donne ainsi satisfaction aux deux sentiments contraires qui peuvent être regardés comme les moteurs par excellence du développement intellectuel : le sentiment de l'obscur et la foi en l'efficacité de l'esprit humain.

Il s'en faut assurément que cette philosophie soit la création personnelle de Taine. Peut-être en pourrait-on trouver les premiers germes chez Aristote. En tout cas, dès le XVIIe siècle, Hobbes la constitua à l'état de système. De lui, l'idée passa en partie à Spinoza et c'est de Spinoza que Taine paraît l'avoir reçue.[1] Il n'y a même pas ajouté grand' chose. La théorie de l'abstraction et de la substitution se retrouve déjà chez Hobbes. Mais il lui a donné une forme populaire. Grâce au brillant exposé qu'il en a fait, elle s'est répandue et est ainsi devenue un des facteurs de notre vie philosophique. Enfin et surtout il a eu le très grand mérite d'appliquer ces idées générales à un ordre particulier de phénomènes, je veux dire aux phénomènes psychologiques. Car la psychologie expérimentale, dont il a été le principal initiateur en France, repose précisément sur cet axiome que la conscience n'est pas une réalité aussi simple et aussi facile à connaitre que le supposait l'école introspectionniste; qu'elle ne se réduit pas à un petit groupe

---

1. Comte pourrait être rattaché à la même lignée philosophique. Mais je ne saurais dire dans quelle mesure Taine a pu subir son influence.

bitter. Rationalist empiricism is not exposed to either of these dangers. Even in going as far as empiricism in the domain of science, and even in opening all of the world to free enquiry and affirming that there is a possible explanation of things, it puts in a plea in bar of simple, summary explanations. Without condemning reason to give up, without even setting limits to its future ambitions, it puts it on guard against itself. It gives it the sense of a surrounding darkness, while recognizing its power, little by little, to spread light. It gives satisfaction in this way to two contrary feelings, which can be seen as the great driving forces of intellectual development – the sense of the obscure, and faith in the power of the human mind.

It is of course far from the case that this philosophy was Taine's personal creation. Perhaps the first germs can be found in Aristotle. It was anyway in the 17th century that Hobbes worked it up into a system. From him, the idea passed in part to Spinoza and it is from Spinoza that Taine appears to have taken it.[1] He did not even add much to it. The theory of abstraction and substitution is already to be found in Hobbes. But he gave it a popular form. It is thanks to his brilliant account of it that it spread and so has become one of the factors of our philosophical life. Last but not least, it is to his very great credit that he applied these general ideas to a particular order of phenomena – namely, psychological phenomena. For experimental psychology, which he largely initiated in France, rests precisely on the axiom that the consciousness is not as simple and as easy a reality to know as the introspectionist school assumes; that it does not reduce to a small group of

---

1. Comte could be placed in the same philosophical line. But I cannot tell how far Taine may have come under his influence.

d'idées claires et d'états distincts dont la formule est facile à trouver ; mais qu'elle a, au contraire, des dessous profonds et obscurs et où, pourtant, il n'est pas impossible de faire progressivement descendre la lumière de la raison.

Acceptant pour mon compte les principes fondamentaux de cette philosophie, tels que je viens de les exposer, je suis naturellement porté à apprécier favorablement l'œuvre de Taine. Ce n'est pas que la doctrine n'ait grand besoin d'être refondue et repensée à nouveau par un esprit plus vigoureux, plus apte aux vues d'ensemble et muni d'une culture scientifique beaucoup plus étendue. Taine avait d'ailleurs été trop étroitement en contact avec l'empirisme anglais pour n'en avoir pas fortement subi l'influence : de là des incertitudes et des contradictions dans la suite de ses idées. Esprit analytique, il avait l'ambition des synthèses plus qu'il n'en avait le génie. Même la forme littéraire sous laquelle il exprimait sa pensée ne lui permettait pas une élaboration très approfondie. Ainsi peut-on lui reprocher, non sans raison, d'avoir plutôt juxtaposé que logiquement uni les deux tendances qu'il entreprend de réconcilier. Mais, en dehors d'une doctrine qui les réconcilie, je ne vois pas pour l'esprit d'autre alternative que d'osciller sans fin du simplisme au mysticisme, et inversement. Si donc son entreprise demande à être reprise, il a eu l'honneur de montrer la route où il convient de s'engager.

Si pendant ces temps derniers, elle paraît avoir souffert d'un certain discrédit, c'est pour avoir été mal comprise. On a imputé au système certaines conséquences pratiques qui ne pouvaient pas ne pas alarmer l'opinion. On a dit qu'il aboutissait à une morale qui, sur des points essentiels, contredit celle des honnêtes gens. Mais, en réalité, on n'a pu lui faire tenir le langage qu'on lui a prêté qu'en faussant les principes sur lesquels il repose. Jamais, je crois, Taine, n'eût accepté de regarder la morale comme la simple

clear ideas and distinct states for which it is easy to discover the formula; but that it has, on the contrary, obscure, profound depths which it is not impossible for the light of reason to reach down into more and more.

In accepting for my part the fundamental principles of this philosophy, as I have just set them out, I am naturally led to a favourable assessment of Taine's work. It is not that the approach has no great need to be recast and rethought anew by a more vigorous mind, more capable of an overall view and drawing on a much more extensive scientific culture. Besides, Taine had been in too close contact with English empiricism not to have come very much under its influence: hence the uncertainties and contradictions in the outturn of his ideas. With his analytical mind, he had greater ambition than genius for synthesis. Even the literary form in which he expressed his thought did not allow its in-depth development. Thus the criticism of him can be made, not without reason, that he juxtaposed rather than brought together and logically united the two tendencies which he undertook to reconcile. But, beyond a doctrine which does reconcile them, I see no other alternative for the mind than an endless oscillation, from simplism to mysticism and back again. If, then, there is a need to return to his project, the honour has been his of showing the road to be taken.

If in recent times it seems to have fallen into a certain disrepute, it is because it has been badly understood. Certain practical consequences, attributed to the system, could not fail to alarm public opinion. It has been said that it would lead to a morality going against, on essential points, that of decent people. But, in reality, it can be given the sense ascribed to it only by misrepresenting the principles on which it rests. Taine, I believe, never accepted a view of morality as the simple conclusion of a

conclusion d'un syllogisme dont telle ou telle théorie psychologique ou philosophique aurait fourni les prémisses.

La morale est une réalité vivante et agissante ; c'est un système de faits donnés ; en faire l'étude du point de vue de la science,[a] ce n'est pas chercher à la mettre d'accord avec telle ou telle doctrine métaphysique, c'est l'observer telle qu'elle est et tenter de l'expliquer. C'est se demander quelles sont les causes qui ont donné naissance aux différentes maximes dont elle est faite et quelles en sont les raisons d'être, etc.; puisqu'il s'agit de quelque chose qui est et qui a duré, on peut être certain par avance que ces causes et que ces raisons existent. La réflexion scientifique, si elle est méthodiquement employée, ne peut que les découvrir ; il n'y a donc rien à en redouter. Elle ne peut que nous faire mieux comprendre les préceptes que nous suivons machinalement ou nous aider à les modifier en connaissance de cause, quand il y a lieu, et que des changements sont devenus nécessaires. Cette science, il est vrai, n'est pas faite ; mais tout ce qu'il en faut conclure, c'est qu'il est urgent d'y travailler, non qu'il n'est pas de science qui puisse servir à éclairer la conduite de l'homme. Au lieu de spéculer sur cette lacune au profit du mystère et de l'obscurantisme, il faut chercher à la combler. Telle est la seule attitude qui convienne à des disciples conséquents de cette philosophie. Tant donc qu'on n'aura pas démontré que cette science est impossible — et elle est possible, puisqu'elle a déjà commencé a donner des résultats — la thèse de nos néo-mystiques sera sans fondement. Or, ils ne paraissent pas se douter des recherches qui sont faites dans ce sens. Ils n'ont donc de ce qu'ils attaquent qu'une notion bien confuse. Le héros du *Disciple,* qui a ouvert la campagne il y a environ neuf ans, n'est pas seulement un triste caractère, c'est un médiocre esprit, un mauvais élève qui na pas compris son maître.[b]

syllogism, with this or that psychological or philosophical theory supplying its premises.

Morality is an active, living reality; it is a system of given facts; undertaking its study from the point of view of science is not to seek to make it fit with some metaphysical doctrine or other, but to observe it as it is and to try to explain it. It is to wonder what the causes are which have given rise to the different maxims making it up, and what are its *raisons d'être*, etc.; because it is about something existing and enduring there can be certainty in advance that there are these causes and these reasons. All that scientific enquiry can do, if methodical, is to discover them. There is therefore nothing to fear from it. It can only make for a better understanding of the precepts that we follow unconsciously, or help us to reform them in full knowledge of the case, as circumstances demand and when changes have become necessary. This science, it is true, has not been constructed. But all that it is then right to conclude is that it is urgent to work at it, not that there is no science which could serve to throw light on man's conduct. Instead of speculating on this gap, to the profit of mysteriousness and obscurantism, it is necessary to seek to close it. No other attitude is open to the rational disciple of this philosophy. So until it is shown that this science is impossible – and it is possible, since it has already begun to yield results – the thesis of our neo-mystics lacks foundation. But they do not seem to be aware that research of the kind has been done. They therefore have only a very confused notion of what they attack. The hero of *The Disciple*, who opened the campaign around nine years ago, is not only a sad character, but a second–rate mind, a poor pupil who has not understood his master.[b]

DURKHEIM AND MONTESQUIEU
W. Watts Miller

The Latin thesis is important in two ways. We need to discuss it both as an interpretation of Montesquieu and as a statement of Durkheim's own ideas. Indeed, it is as an interpretation of Montesquieu that it is at the same time a vehicle for these ideas.

I

An interpretation can be more than a commentary. It can be part of how a work inspires another substantive work, that builds on and develops it. This is a reason for valuing "constructivist" readings of a text, that are not just all scholarly exegesis, but that apply the insights of a Durkheim, engaged in the live issues of an area of theory and research. It is also a reason for attributing the first "sociological" interpretation of Montesquieu to Ferguson, in his *Essay on the History of Civil Society*.[1] Or later on there is Constant (a student at Edinburgh while Ferguson was still teaching there), for example in *Ancient and Modern Liberty*,[2] or Tocqueville, in *Democracy in America*.[3] A whole tradition of enquiry precedes the famous "sociological" interpretation of Montesquieu in Comte's commentary on him.

---

1. Ferguson 1767. For a discussion, including the connexion with Montesquieu, see Janet 1887: II, 563-572 (a work used and cited by Durkheim).

2. Constant [1819] 1980. On the connexion, see, e.g. Sorel 1887: 161 and Benrekassa 1987: 192-194.

3. Tocqueville 1835-1840. On the connexion, see, e.g., Janet 1887: II, 736-738; Sorel 1887: 166-167; Benrekassa 1987: 193-194.

Of course, it was in this discussion of Montesquieu that Comte introduced and defined the very term, "sociology".[1] Let us nonetheless use it in a broad–church way. Let us also, now, keep just to commentaries. Then Comte might have been the first to suggest and sketch in a "sociological" interpretation of *The Spirit of the Laws*. Durkheim was the first to develop and fill one out.

This is evident from a comparison with other commentaries of the period. Sainte-Beuve offers bright but disgruntled dinner–table chatter for aristocrats.[2] Laboulaye, after a long introduction to *The Spirit of the Laws* in the only edition of the *Collected Works* produced in Durkheim's time, buries his own thoughts and observations in the notes.[3] Taine distills Comte in a brief, incisive passage, to emphasize Montesquieu's concern with system but lack of an idea of progress.[4] Flint takes a ponderous chapter to do the same.[5] Zévort is banale.[6] Faguet is unrelieved, college course–book tedium.[7] There are only two works of much relevance and use. Durkheim cites the one by Janet,[8] and ignores the other which, with its polish, can seem less substantial, by Sorel.[9]

---

1. Comte 1839: IV, 200-201.

2. Sainte-Beuve 1853: VII, 33-66.

3. See, especially, the last section of his introduction, Laboulaye 1876: III, lxvii-lxix. For a discussion of Laboulaye, see Goyard-Fabre 1993: 328-342.

4. Taine 1877: I, 234-235.

5. Flint 1874: 93-108.

6. Zévort 1887.

7. Faguet 1890: 137-192.

8. The core of this account of Montesquieu first appeared in Janet 1858: II, 338-450. It was added to, rather than revised (with the work as a whole retitled), in the 2nd edn., Janet 1872: II, 417-556 – and again in the 3rd edn., 1887: II, 303-405, 465-477. This is the one used by Durkheim, and the relevant pagination is the same as in the 4th edn., 1913.

9. Sorel 1887.

The Latin thesis soon turned up on reference lists on Montesquieu, even if it does not seem to have been read or absorbed by the authors of them.[1] It was also privately translated by Alengry in the 1890s, as he points out in a note introducing the publication of that translation in 1937.[2] Again, however, the thesis does not seem to have had an impact on the burgeoning literature on Montesquieu between these years. This is despite much talk of a "sociological" Montesquieu, not just by Alengry,[3] but also, for example, by Dedieu[4] and Brunschvicg.[5] Even in 1939, in an important, more or less sociologically oriented collection of articles on Montesquieu by Davy, Hubert and Gurvitch, the only reference to Durkheim is by Gurvitch.[6] It is difficult to believe, in the case of some of these writers, that they were unacquainted with the Latin thesis, even in the original, or in no way influenced by it. Moreover, Alengry says that his translation was seen and approved of by Durkheim himself, and it might well have circulated within the Durkheimian circle, who, Alengry also says, put great pressure on him to publish it.

But Durkheim's Montesquieu did not really acquire prominence until after the war, in an upsurge of interest in Montesquieu himself, and perhaps in an effort, like Durkheim's own, to reassert a French heritage. It did so

---

1. See, e.g., Archambault, n.d.; Dedieu 1913; Hémon, n.d. Durkheim is no more than a bibliographical entry in Hémon and Dedieu. His table of societies is reproduced in Archambault (n.d.: 28), who sees him as dating sociology from Montesquieu's work, but also as stressing two key ideas in it, "celle de genre et celle de fin"! (*ibid.*: 47), which should of course be "celle de genre et celle de loi".

2. Alengry 1937: 405-406.

3. Alengry 1900: 389-403.

4. Dedieu 1913: 60-100 (on Montesquieu's "sociological method").

5. Brunschvicg 1927: II, 489-501 (on Montesquieu's "sociology of progress").

6. Gurvitch 1939: 611-612, 625. *Cf.* Davy 1939; Hubert 1939.

mainly through Davy's paper at a 1948 conference,[1] Brethe de la Gressaye's introduction to a new, influential edition of *The Spirit of the Laws* in 1950,[2] and Cuvillier's translation of the thesis in 1953.[3] It was only then that it entered the canon, to become a much discussed, almost obligatory, and as if long recognized reference.

II

But have we now reached the stage at which it is a museum piece – important only for its historical interest? Yet as well as being about Montesquieu, it is about social science. So there are two questions, rather than one.

The first is if it has not been long overtaken by works of scholarship in search, as it were, of a "Montesquieuan" Montesquieu. There are many such studies. Perhaps the most authoritative remains Shackleton's.[4]

The second question is if it has not been long overtaken by contemporary versions of a "sociological" Montesquieu. The best-known examples of these are the essays by Althusser and Aron.[5]

Durkheim, as he himself emphasizes in the conclusion to the thesis, sets out to grasp Montesquieu's work in its essentials and to focus on what seems his outstanding

---

1. Davy 1949: 127-171.

2. Brethe de la Gressaye 1950: I, xcv-c. There is also much talk of a "sociological" Montesquieu, without invoking Durkheim, in Caillois 1949: I, xiii-xvi. This is in the introduction to the first edition of Montesquieu's *Complete Works* since Laboulaye's. But, in the new climate, its effect is to invoke Durkheim. See also Cotta 1953.

3. He implies it is new, rather than done some time before, in criticizing Alengry's translation and justifying the need for a new one. See Cuvillier 1953: 25 , n. 1.

4. Shackleton 1961.

5. Althusser 1959; Aron 1967.

achievement. Accordingly:

(1) He makes no attempt to go into the history of ideas in detail – something done at the time by Janet. He is therefore open to the criticism that he oversimplifies things to the point of distortion.[1]

(2) He makes no attempt to situate Montesquieu within the politics of the old regime – something done at the time by Janet and Sorel.[2] He is therefore silent on a much debated issue nowadays, as in Althusser's view that Montesquieu's social theory is progressive *qua* science, but reactionary in its politics and ideological tenor and implications.[3]

(3) He makes little or no attempt, in his focus on *The Spirit of the Laws,* to draw on Montesquieu's other work as a help with its interpretation. But, even if he had tried, so much that is now drawn on by scholars was then unavailable, including the writings published in nine volumes between 1891 and 1914, as well as other material published during that period and since.[4]

So in a number of ways, to do with the contextualization of *The Spirit of the Laws,* Durkheim has long been out of the running – but partly because he never wanted to be in it. The same can be said about the plan and arrangement of *The Spirit of the Laws,* a topic discussed by generations of commentators.[5] Durkheim refuses to become drawn into

---

1. E.g., that he distorts Montesquieu's break with natural law theorists of the period, in completely ignoring their interest both in sociohistorical diversity and in empirical investigation. See Waddicor 1970: 33-35, 102.

2. Janet 1887: II, 361-365; Sorel 1887: 142-148.

3. Althusser 1959: 103-116. See, in reponse, Aron 1967: 62-63, and, e.g., in comment on both, Benrekassa 1987: 141-144.

4. See note on editions, Caillois 1949: I, xxxv.

5. See, e.g., Vernière 1977: 51-97, who excludes the final, historical books from an overall design/plan. For a persuasive integrationist view of them, see Shackleton 1961: 320-336.

detailed argument over this, and instead just gets on with an idea of the work's essential coherence.

Let us now turn to a key claim in his interpretation of it as a work of sociology. It is that in order to investigate laws, Montesquieu investigates social phenomena as a whole – in the sense both of all or almost all of them, and of their connectedness in a totality. This allows for a focus on Montesquieu's concern with laws – or with morals or with politics or whatever – but rules out losing sight of his "sociological" concern with the relationship of each of these with all the others, and in a totality.

Then it is just a very basic interpretation of Montesquieu which is very difficult to dispute. It is irrelevant if it goes back long before Durkheim to someone else,[1] or to nobody in particular. It is still a key interpretive claim which has not been overtaken by modern scholarship, since this has little if any reason to challenge it. The same seems true of the subsidiary claim, that it is Montesquieu's wide–ranging, holistic interest that helps to make him original.[2]

The picture changes, of course, once we try to elaborate on the interest, and let us begin with the issue of whether or not it is a holism of essentially static social systems.

Durkheim can seem very dated, because he *complains* that Montesquieu does not have a notion of progress. Aron can seem very modern, since he more or less *praises* him for not having one.[3] But both share the view, that he does indeed lack such a notion, and it is a view that has long been challenged. Montesquieu's work clearly involves an idea of progress, according to Brunschvicg,[4] or at least he

---

1. Hegel is nominated by Benrekassa 1987: 96.

2. A claim stressed by Althusser 1959: 7-9, and uncontested even by Waddicor 1970: 35-36.

3. Aron 1967: 66.

4. Brunschwicg 1927: II, 501.

has a complex, ambivalent attitude, according to Hubert,[1] and there is again complexity, ambivalence, nuance, according to Benrekassa – who, provided the idea of progress is so understood, also seems to revive support for belief in it.[2]

What about the concern in *The Spirit of the Laws* with history, not merely as a chronicle of events, but as an account of underlying dynamics and long–term processes of change? It is something of an omission that Durkheim completely ignores the final books, on the development of the French monarchy. More mysteriously, he combines the claim, made at one point, that Montesquieu has an essentially static view of each of his types as a system, with recognition, elsewhere, of his interest in dynamics and change. It is also a claim made, at one point, by Sorel[3] – despite going on to discuss the final, historical books.[4] And perhaps the claim's most effective dismissal is at the hands of Althusser – yet not through appeal to these books. It is through appeal to Montesquieu's dynamic view of systems themselves. This looks beyond their nature, in the sense of structure, to their animating principle, in a concern with processes of their corruption or collapse – which above all involve, for Althusser, a "contradiction" between structure and principle.[5] But it is here, too, that Durkheim's Montesquieu comes to life, through concern with the dynamic at work in a sociohistorical system.

This is in a set of claims which are each a key part of his "sociological" interpretation, and which together make it distinctive. One is that Montesquieu's classification is not

---

1. Hubert 1939: 610.
2. Benrekassa 1987: 177-185.
3. Sorel 1887: 87-88.
4. *Ibid.*: 128-134.
5. Althusser 1959: 45.

of governments, but of societies. Another is that his theory of interconnectedness is not just multifactorial, but essentialist – some things are more important than others in defining and shaping a society, and constitute, in this sense, its nature. Another translates Montesquieu's talk of corruption into concern with a society's "deviation" from its nature and so from the "normal". Then all of this links up with the development of what might be called Durkheim's "internalist programme".[1] He asks how, according to Montesquieu, a society can deviate from its own nature, and criticizes his reliance on "accidental", "external" causes. The criticism may or may not be unfair. The point remains that, just as we should root a society's ideals in the society itself, we should try to find an explanation of its pathologies in causes that are part of its nature too, even in working against and threatening to collapse it.

However, let us return to the view that Montesquieu's classification is not of governments but of societies. This was certainly a distinctive interpretation at the time. Janet and Sorel remain locked in a focus on governments. Nowadays, however, it has become common to defend Montesquieu's departure from a traditional scheme, in an approach that embeds government in a wider political sociology. But this does not quite take us from politics and a study of governments to sociology and a study of societies themselves. Perhaps Shackleton does take us there, when he says that Montesquieu *replaces* a conventional enumeration of governments with "a classification of societies according to their mode of life".[2] His discussion still concentrates on Montesquieu's "theory

---

1. See Watts Miller 1996: 2-4 (where the term is introduced, with subsequent discussion).
2. Shackleton 1961: 267.

of governments", even if a theory of societies is the essential background. How, with Durkheim, is the picture different?

For a start, he brings out Montesquieu's interest in the modes of life of hunters and pastoralists. This is an interest in societies that are unconnected with any form of state, since they are societies that do not have a state. It was soon taken up and developed in Ferguson's "sociological" interpretation of Montesquieu – in an emphasis on such societies noted, rather disapprovingly, by Janet,[1] but just ignored by Durkheim, though he read Janet and complains that these societies are just ignored by Montesquieu's interpreters. They are still to a large extent ignored today, failing to turn up in Althusser, Aron, Benrekassa, Shackleton, Vernière, etc. [2]

Let us now go on to societies that do have states. Here, Durkheim comes up with a radical "sociological" interpretation of Montesquieu in two main ways. One involves looking beyond the structure and principle of a type of *government*, to find the structure and principle (renamed the "social tie") of a type of *society*. The other marginalizes government itself, in excluding it from the dynamic social core of things.

Durkheim begins by identifying the republic with the ancient city–state. But in going on to look for its social structure and principle, he identifies the first with a basic homogeneity, the second with the group–attachments of a powerful and extensive *conscience commune*. So in effect he assimilates the republic (along with stateless societies) as a particular case of a general type – described as traditional

---

1. Janet 1887: II, 564, 566-567, 571-572.

2. But they turn up, via Durkheim, in Archambault, n.d.: 27, and also, of course, in more anthropologically minded discussions – see, e.g., on Ferguson's development of Montesquieu, Meek 1976: 150-155.

"segmentary" or "mechanical" society in his main thesis, the *Division of Labour*. So does he also rework Montesquieu's account of monarchies as an account of what the main thesis sees as modern "organic" society?

He characterizes their social structure in terms of the division of labour, which he moves into place as the basic constitutive, organizing pattern of the modern world – and it is of interest that Ferguson's "sociological" interpretation of Montesquieu does the same.

But Durkheim seems to falter – again like Ferguson – over the social principle. He seems still to be working his way from an ethic of honour, which is not at all just the other side of self–interest yet can be corrupted into it, to an ethic of everyone's freedom and dignity as a person ("the human ideal"), which is not at all a narrow individualism yet can be corrupted into it. Or at least this is the case in the Latin thesis. In the main thesis, the division of labour and the human ideal take their place as a Montesquieuan structure and principle, that together constitute the core dynamic of modern society.

We also need to bring in Durkheim's other writings to assess his campaign, in the Latin thesis, against exaggerated views of the importance of government. It is not just that he criticizes Montesquieu's use of forms of government to name types of society. Nor is it just that he says, as if out to shock, that Montesquieu would not have considered modern France a republic. It is that he goes very much further when he denies – perhaps thinking of all the regimes that had come and gone in France since the Revolution – any definite connexion between types of government and types of society.

Then this goes against his whole approach and interest in a dynamic that shapes a society's institutions – including its institutions of government – but that is a source, too, of

corrupt, pathological forms of these. In fact, the issue of government is important in the development of his internalist programme, and occupies a central place in a lecture–course that was given in the 1890s, and that involves worries about a contemporary political malaise, a search for Montesquieuan "intermediate groups", and an ideal of modern, "true" democracy.[1]

Moreover, it is his general approach which can address the point that Montesquieu does not just work with the typology, *republic, monarchy* and *despotism,* but introduces another, of *free, moderate* and *despotic* governments.[2]

A Durkheimian view of the first as essentially sociological clears the ground for a view of the second as essentially political, and for enquiry into connexions between each of these kinds of society and of government. It is a way out of the muddles of a treatment which concentrates on both as accounts of government. In saying, as if out to shock, that Montesquieu would not have considered France a republic, Durkheim is probably getting at Janet, who says, in shocked tones, that Montesquieu would not have considered America a republic – when, on the contrary, it is a modern exemplar of freedom and democracy.[3] Sorel, appealing both to France and America, says similar things.[4] The deeper issue, of course, is how the modern world, to the extent that it is "monarchical" in its society, can nonetheless realize its own "republican" aspirations to free, democratic government. It was soon articulated, in the Montesquieuan tradition, in the work of Constant and Tocqueville. It remains a central, underlying issue in commentaries today, and ties up, not only with the

---

1. Durkheim 1950a.
2. See, e.g., Vernière 1977: 70. *Cf.* Janet 1887: II, 364-377.
3. Janet 1887: II, 377-378.
4. Sorel 1887: 93-97.

theory of the division of powers, but with the theme of despotism.

The Latin thesis treats – and defends – *despotism* as an account both of a real type of society and a real type of government, in which religion is the source of the ruler's power and so also the force that curbs and limits it. Such an interpretation is too easily dismissed in the view that Montesquieu's despotism is a "spectre", dressed up *à la turque,* but in fact Louis XIV and the modern western absolutist state in disguise. In any case, Durkheim obviously knew about this view, partly because he would have read it in Janet,[1] and did not have to wait until Althusser, Aron or whoever. [2] But it is also because it is a worry over despotism he shared himself.

His first publication identifies a modern dilemma: either there is a "conflict of unfettered egoisms", rooted in individualism and generating an oppressive, class–divided society, or, in reaction, there is a concentration of power in a "despotic socialism".[3] The Latin thesis calls despotism a "monstrosity".[4] The new edition of *The Division of Labour* repeats this language, warning that a mass of unorganized individuals lets in "the sociological monstrosity" of an authoritarian, overmighty state.[5] And, as before, Durkheim looks for a solution in new forms of Montesquieuan intermediate groups – that link individuals with the wider society, that draw them into active citizenship, that entrench commitment to the human ideal, and that spread power around, in counter–balancing and sharing it.

---

1. Janet 1887: II, 365.
2. Althusser 1959: 86; Aron 1967: 37.
3. Durkheim 1885a: 96.
4. Durkheim 1892a: 39-40.
5. Durkheim 1902b: xxxii.

So let us now consider the discussion, in the Latin thesis, of the "famous" theory of the division of powers. This connects it with the division of labour, to insist that it is only an expression of Montesquieu's general theory of modern society. It can therefore seem only another expression of Durkheim's own general interpretive project, to shift focus from Montesquieu's interest in government to his interest in society. Yet it contains the basis for a return, as in Durkheim's other work, to the interest in government.

It is not to follow Althusser, in an outright rejection of Montesquieuan politics as reactionary. But it is not to settle, either, for vague talk of pluralism and what have been called Aron's "liberal banalities".[1] It is a search for the particular kinds of intermediate groups that are possible in the modern world, that can counteract its egoistic, authoritarian and other systematic pathologies, and that are necessary if there is to be anything like the ethical commonwealth of persons demanded by its own human ideal.

III

Durkheim's main thesis, on the division of labour, is primarily a work of substantive social theory. His subsidiary thesis also involves this, as is clear from the discussion so far. But it is primarily a work on the philosophy and methodology of social science.

Indeed, this is perhaps the main reason for its continuing importance, both as an interpretation of Montesquieu and as a statement of Durkheim's own ideas. It explores, in an engagement with one great, original and difficult thinker by another, a whole range of issues which underlie the

---

1. Benrekassa 1987: 144.

substantive social theorization and enquiry of both, and which remain fundamental to the project of social science.

These issues include rationalism versus empiricism,[1] individualism versus holism,[2] varieties of explanation and the nature of causality as necessary connexion,[3] determinism and freedom,[4] "factual" sociological versus "evaluative" philosophical concerns,[5] etc. They inevitably break loose, to some extent, from the structure within which Durkheim sets out to develop and organize his discussion of them. It is essentially the same structure as in *The Rules of Sociological Method,* going from the subject–matter of social science to classification, then explanation, then method. Instead of simply keeping to this order, let us reverse it, and start with method.

We then hit, straightaway, the issue of rationalism versus empiricism. But we should also notice, straight-away, that Durkheim opposes attempts to set up a false dichotomy, as if a choice must be made between two extreme positions. Instead he subscribes to what he calls, in the article on Taine, "rationalist empiricism". Indeed, this article sets out very clearly views put into practice in *Suicide* (published the same year), developed in *The Rules,* and going back to the Latin thesis itself.

Durkheim is committed to an empirical detective–work which goes to observable phenomena in a search, via induction, for general, persistent patterns of these and for regular, law–like connexions between them. But this is in turn in a search for underlying realities which we might infer, via deduction, that they disclose, and for a rationale

---

1. See, e.g., Jones 1994: 1-39.
2. See, e.g., Fraisse 1989: 195-219.
3. See, e.g., Schmaus 1995: 57-75; Watts Miller 1996: 47-71.
4. See, e.g., Watts Miller 1997: 223-235.
5. See, e.g., Gentile 1975.

which we might grasp, again via deduction, as an intelligible, necessary logic at work in things.

A development of all this is in the chapter on method in *The Rules*. Durkheim attacks J. S. Mill, to stress the role of deduction in science, but also that empirical detective–work in sociology can concentrate on a single method, that of concomitant variation. Yet how? Mill's empiricism limits science to the investigation of regularly connected phenemona, and so needs a whole array of statistical techniques to try to pick out which things are nonetheless, in some sense, "causes" of others. It might be wondered if this in fact smuggles in an idea of cause involving intelligible, necessary connexions. It is in any case in insisting on these that Durkheim emphasizes a particular kind of detective–work, but within a web of theoretical, interpretive–deductive reasoning, to try to pick out and understand real causal processes.[1]

In the case of the Latin thesis, it is clear that Durkheim accepts the idea of laws as "necessary connexions which follow from the nature of things", and although he does not discuss the idea of a *spirit* of the laws, it also seems clear that he understands and accepts it as a social world's core logic, tending to shape other things to develop in line with it. An issue is then the kinds of explanation this entails. As Vernière, supported by Beyer, puts it, "*The Spirit of the Laws* involves a double dynamic, the search for causes and the discovery of a finality".[2]

Durkheim's interpretation is the same. But although he endorses the search for causes in what he calls efficient explanation, he is critical of teleology or, as he calls it, final explanation. This is partly because he identifies it with

---

1. Durkheim [1895a/1901c] 1947a: 155-162.
2. Vernière 1977: 57; Beyer 1982: 379-381.

versions serving up the idea of a society constituted according to a legislator's conscious design. But it is also because he identifies other versions with the limitations of functional explanation, which cannot say whether or not a need will be met, only that ways of meeting it, if they develop, tend to stay in place.[1] According to a key passage, final explanation concerns the "means which the nature of society requires to realize itself, that is, to achieve its end; but these might be lacking".[2] Yet this overlooks the power and point of final explanation when it invokes – as in *The Division of Labour* itself – a *spirit* of the laws, that tends to shape social institutions, and to bring about the "means" it needs for its development. There is a "double dynamic" – of a finality in which something crucially explains what happens in particular social worlds because it constitutes their nature and self–realizing *telos,* and of an efficiency in which it constitutes their nature and self-realizing *telos* because it crucially explains what happens in them.

This does not mean that a society's core, underlying rationale is all–powerful, or cannot run into trouble and even face collapse. On the contrary, it takes us to Durkheim's criticism that Montesquieu tries to explain a society's problems and pathologies through reliance on contingent, external causes, lying outside its nature, instead of trying to find causes lying within it.[3] This might be unfair, given Montesquieu's concern with despotism, not in far–off lands, but as an ever–present possibility built into the modern world. Yet even if it is an unfair, it is a theoretically fruitful criticism, in helping to bring out the challenges and demands of an internalist programme. It is

1. Durkheim 1892a: 53.
2. *Ibid.*: 51.
3. *Ibid.*: 53-56

not enough, as Durkheim seems tempted to do in *The Division of Labour,* to try to keep a logic "pure", so that it is a force only for the realization of our society's ideals, and is without responsibility for its malaise. Nor is it enough to identify a rationale that secretes the pathologies, but that fails to explain the values critical of them and of our existing society. Somehow, perhaps as Montesquieu tries to do in *The Spirit of the Laws,* and as Durkheim eventually manages to do in *Suicide,* the internalist programme must find an ambivalent "double dynamic", that is a source both of our ills and of our ideals.[1]

Let us now consider an issue which cuts all the way through explanation, classification and the subject matter of social science. Indeed, it generates an argument against the very idea of a social science, and so, it might seem, against the very projects of Montesquieu and Durkheim. This is that, far from being made up of things that call for "explanation", the social world is all significance and meaning, and so calls for "interpretation".

In the first place, however, the argument generally assumes a positivist view of causal explanation, accepting this for the natural world but rejecting its extension to the social world. So it fails against Montesquieu and Durkheim – who work with a different view, in their search for the intelligible, necessary connexions of a social world's rationale, and, in the article on Taine, Durkheim himself protests against a positivism that, "extends to everything, (but) enlightens nothing", and "spreads mystery everywhere".[2]

Moreover, both explanation and interpretation are involved in Durkheim's concern, that so attracts him to

---

1. For a fuller discussion, see Watts Miller 1996.
2. Durkheim [1897f], in this edition: 78.

Montesquieu, with the investigation of different types of
societies and their institutions in a comparative social
science. It is essential to explain things in a particular,
individual society in terms of a wider, comparative run of
data. But Durkheim always opposes indiscriminate,
encyclopaedic collections of "facts". Things must be
interpreted in context, both in relation to other societies of
a similar kind, and, in the same society, as interconnected
parts of a whole.

Finally, the world studied by social science is clearly in
some sense mind–dependent. In *The Rules,* it "consists
entirely of representations".[1] In the opening list in the
Latin thesis, it consists of "laws, morals, religions, etc."
But these, though mind–dependent, are still "things".
Why?

"Things", as first defined in the thesis, "have their own
characteristics and therefore require sciences able to
describe and explain these".[2] And a constant Durkheimian
theme is that the ideas and relations involved in social life,
far from being all transparence, are complex, tangled and
obscure. Hence the emphasis on them as "things", in the
sense of requiring an empirical, scientific enquiry to
investigate their meanings, track their implications and
connexions, and uncover an underlying logic at work in
them. This is in a campaign against two views, that seem
the alternatives to empirical social science, even if they are
not what its critics, nowadays, might want to come out and
say they support. One is the homespun notion that whatever
is mind–dependent is accessible just through introspection.
The other is a grander metaphysics in which, as in the

1. Durkheim [1901c] 1947a: xi. For one of the best recent accounts of
Durkheim on "representations", "things" and "reality", see Stedman Jones
1996: 43-60.
2. Durkheim 1892a: 11.

article on Taine: "Since the world is something thought, thought, just by its own powers, must be able to reconstruct it".[1]

But Durkheim also has a second definition of "things", in which, as in the Latin thesis, they "have their own stable nature and a power to resist human will."[2] So a crucial, but often overlooked point about Durkheimian social science is that it is about *mind–dependent* yet at the same time *will–independent* things. This does not mean that they resist change altogether. Nor does it mean that they resist only the will of individuals – despite the preoccupation, in *The Rules,* with societal "constraint" of the individual. The more thoroughgoing argument of the thesis is that the deeply engrained beliefs, practices and logic of a social world also resist change at will collectively. It is possible to have reform. What is not possible is a wand–waving creation of a completely new and different society, something Montesquieu is praised for understanding,[3] and which is also a message of *The Division of Labour.*[4]

Lurking in all this there are questions about determinism and freedom – a problem that bothered Durkheim, even or especially in his many protests that it did not, and he claims, in the Latin thesis, that it also did not concern Montesquieu. The claim focuses on Montesquieu's introduction of a capacity to deviate from a law–governed order of things, and at the very least embarrasses its interpretation as an interest in how to introduce freewill. For it involves, as Durkheim says, a general interest in some such capacity not only amongst humans, but amongst animals and even, perhaps, plants. So it involves, as he

---

1. Durkheim [1897f], in this edition: 76.
2. Durkheim 1892a: 20.
3. *Ibid.*: 22, 51.
4. Durkheim [1893b] 1902b: xli.

goes on to argue, a general question about the normal and abnormal, and, as he goes on to complain, quoting Zeller, a traditional, Aristotelian view that limits explanation in terms of a law–governed order to the normal, and banishes everything else to a mysterious realm of the accidental and contingent.

Nor, we might add, is this a very promising place to look for human freedom of the will, if it is an affair of the rational, and not merely the arbitrary. Then if we return to Durkheim's own argument, and so to his internalist programme's search to explain not only the normal but the abnormal in terms of the same thing – a social world's essential nature and rationale – this is also the place to search for freedom or, as he says in *The Division of Labour* and elsewhere,[1] autonomy of the will.

In a way, this takes us well beyond the thesis on Montesquieu to Durkheim's engagement with Kant, and other discussions try to explain how he reworks Kantian autonomy but also how, like Kant, he attempts to combine freewill and necessary connexion.[2] Yet it is in his engagement, in the Latin thesis, with Montesquieu that he develops an essential basis of his approach to these problems.

The same is true if we turn, finally, to an issue of life-long importance to him, the relationship between science and ethics, or, as he often talks of it, "art". Rosso has a point when he says that although Montesquieu clearly has a sociology, sociologists who nowadays wanted to follow his example would be disqualified, since he is at one and the same time a moralist.[3] But it is not just that a "value–free"

---

1. See esp. Durkheim 1925a – a course of lectures on moral education probably first given in 1898-1899.
2. Watts Miller 1996 and 1997.
3. Rosso 1971: 28.

social science disconnects itself from ethics. It is also that philosophers disconnect themselves from social science, in an ideal of a "fact–free" ethics, independent (and ignorant) of anthropology and history. And though they happily read Kant, how many of them bother with Montesquieu?

For Montesquieu, in *The Spirit of the Laws,* does ethics through social science, so that to try to keep the ethics and throw out the social science would be to be left with a meaningless, empty shell. It is the same with Ferguson's *Essay on the History of Civil Society,* Tocqueville's *Democracy in America,* and Durkheim's *Division of Labour* and *Suicide.*

It is true that Durkheim complains about Montesquieu:

> He does not go into what is the case in one part of his work, what ought to be in another, but art and science are so mixed together that there is often an almost impreceptible shift from one to the other.[1]

But this is disingenuous. Durkheim always wants a science of morals that is the route to ethics, and so must find a bridge between them, discovered, in the thesis on Montesquieu, in the idea of the normal as fit with a social world's dynamic and rationale. Then even if a discussion concentrates on the normal from the perspective of a scientific, explanatory interest and makes no attempt to bring out its implications from the perspective of an ethical, evaluative interest, it inevitably contains such implications. Looking for them is the whole point of looking to the normal as a bridge between moral science and moral art.

But why does Durkheim hold, as a basic ethical principle, that the real and its rationale are the good? It is possible, through literature, history and the social sciences,

---

2. Durkheim 1892a: 23.

to reach out of our situation to try to understand other social worlds very different from our own. But a power to imagine these is not the same as a power to will them. And a long–running Durkheimian argument is that what we can will is very much rooted in our situation, attachments and identity. Yet if these lie at the source of the will, there remains a need to illuminate and guide it. And so there is the Durkheimian argument for understanding of the modern social world's underlying dynamic, and for acceptance of the ideal of the person, in a society of persons, that he sees at the heart of this.

Yet Durkheim's social science and ethics are not simply relativist. In questioning Montesquieu's idea of somehow "antecedent" relations of justice, Durkheim still accepts a search for universals, and in fact undertakes this himself in the lectures in moral education, in a concern with essential features of morality in all times and places. But the concern, shared with Montesquieu, with different kinds of societies, rationales and dynamics, is also in a way to do with a universal, even, perhaps, the most important of all. For it is a sociological and ethical appeal in these different worlds to the same *thing,* their *spirit* of the laws.

NOTES

p. 7 **a.** Comte introduced the term in his own discussion of Montesquieu:

Depuis Montesquieu, le seul pas important qu'ait fait jusqui'ici la conception fondamentale de la *sociologie*(1) est dû à l'illustre et malheureux Condorcet.

After Montesquieu, the only important advance that was then made in the fundamental conception of *sociology*(1) was due to the famous and unfortunate Condorcet.

(1) Je crois devoir hasarder, dès à présent, ce terme nouveau, exactement équivalent à mon expression, déjà introduite, de *physique sociale,* afin de pouvoir désigner par un nom unique cette partie complémentaire de la philosophie naturelle qui se rapporte à l'étude positive de l'ensemble des lois fondamentales propres aux phénomènes sociaux. (Comte, *Cours de philosophie positive, IV* [1839]: 200-201)

(1) I believe the risk must be taken of using, from now on, this new term – the exact equivalent of the expression, *social physics,* that I have already introduced – so as to be able to designate with a unique name this part of natural philosophy, relating to the positive study of the totality of fundamental laws specific to social phenomena.

b. *Secundatus* translates the family name, rather than the title, of Charles Secondat, baron de Montesquieu.

CHAPTER 1

p. 11 **a.** The text is ambiguous between (1) science can aim only at description and explanation, which requires a basis in a definite subject matter, and (2) it cannot go on to aim at other things as well, without such a basis. Durkheim must intend (2), in going on to argue for science both in its own right and as the key to ethics.

p. 12 **a.** Corrected to *detineat,* instead of the original text's *destineat.* The correction is suggested by Cuvillier, p. 31, n. 1.

p. 16 **a.** Πολιτεία has two senses in Aristotle. One refers to the political order, commonwealth or state as such. The other refers to a particular form of state, here translated as "republic", in line with its translation as "république" in Janet's *Histoire de la science politique* (1887: I, 211-13) – a work much cited by Durkheim. Aristotle introduces his classification of governments in the following passage:

καλεῖν δ' εἰώθαμεν τῶν μὲν μοναρχιῶν τὴν πρὸς τὸ κοινὸν ἀποβλέπουσαν συμφέρον βασιλείαν, τὴν δὲ τῶν ὀλίγων μὲν πλειόνων δὲ ἑνὸς ἀριστοκρατίαν (ἢ διὰ τὸ τοὺς ἀρίστους ἄρχειν, ἢ διὰ τὸ πρὸς τὸ ἄριστον τῇ πόλει καὶ τοῖς κοινωνοῦσιν αὐτῆς), ὅταν δὲ τὸ πλῆθος πρὸς τὸ κοινὸν πολιτεύηται συμφέρον, καλεῖται τὸ κοινὸν ὄνομα πασῶν τῶν πολιτειῶν, πολιτεία...

παρεκβάσεις δὲ τῶν εἰρημένων τυραννὶς μὲν βασιλείας, ὀλιγαρχία δὲ ἀριστοκρατίας, δημοκρατία δὲ πολιτείας. ἡ μὲν γὰρ τυραννίς ἐστι μοναρχία πρὸς τὸ συμφέρον τὸ τοῦ μοναρχοῦντος, ἡ δ' ὀλιγαρχία πρὸς τὸ τῶν εὐπόρων, ἡ δὲ δημοκρατία πρὸς τὸ συμφέρον τὸ τῶν ἀπόρων· πρὸς δὲ τὸ τῷ κοινῷ λυσιτελοῦν οὐδεμία αὐτῶν.
(Aristotle, *Politics*, III.7)

We usually call rule by monarchs, when directed towards the common good, kingship, just as we call rule by more than one person, but by a few, aristocracy – either because it is rule by the best persons or because they rule with a view to what is best for the city and for its members – and when the people govern with a view to the common good it is called by the term common to all states, a republic...

The forms that deviate from these are tyranny from kingship, oligarchy from aristocracy, and democracy from a republic. Tyranny is monarchy concerned with the interest of the monarch, oligarchy is concerned with the interest of the rich, democracy with the interest of the poor; none of them is concerned with the common good.

p. 18 **a.** The reference corresponds with pp. xxxvii-xxxviii, in the 1902 and subsequent editions of *The Division of Labour*.

CHAPTER 2

p. 22   **a.** Here, and at later points, Durkheim quotes from the following passage (with a phrase he interestingly translates underlined):

Ceux qui auront quelques lumières verront du premier coup d'œil que *[p. 22, n. 1]* cet ouvrage a pour objet les lois, les coutumes et les divers usages de tous les peuples de la terre. On peut dire que le sujet en est immense, puisqu'il embrasse toutes les institutions qui sont reçues parmi les hommes ; puisque l'auteur distingue ces institutions ; *[p. 23, n. 5]* qu'il examine celles qui conviennent le plus à la société, et à chaque société ; *[p. 22, n. 2]* qu'il en cherche l'origine ; qu'il en découvre les causes physiques et morales ; *[p. 23, n. 5]* qu'il examine celles qui ont un degré de bonté par elles-mêmes, et celles qui n'en ont aucun ; que de deux pratiques pernicieuses, il cherche celle qui l'est plus et celle qui l'est moins.

(Défense de l'Esprit des Lois)

Those in search of knowledge will see right away that *[p. 22, n. 1]* this work deals with the laws, customs and different practices of all the peoples of the earth. It may be said that its subject is vast, since it covers all the institutions in force amongst human beings; since the author distinguishes these institutions; *[p. 23, n. 5]* he examines those which best suit society in general and each society; *[p. 22, n. 2]* he seeks their origins; he discovers their physical and moral causes; *[p. 23, n. 5]* he investigates which are of some benefit in themselves and which are of none; he sets out to find, in the case of two practices that are harmful, which is more so, which less.

p. 23   **a.** The passage, with underlining of a phrase Durkheim omits, is:

Je n'écris point pour censurer ce qui est établi dans quelque pays que ce soit. Chaque nation trouvera ici les raisons de ses maximes...

I do not write to condemn what is established in any land whatsoever. Each nation will find here the explanation of its maxims...

Si je pouvais faire en sorte que tout le monde eût de nouvelles raisons pour aimer ses devoirs, son prince, sa patrie, ses lois ; qu'on pût mieux sentir son bonheur dans chaque pays, dans chaque Gouvernement, dans chaque poste où l'on se trouve, je me croirais le plus heureux des mortels. (*L'Esprit des lois,* préface)

If I could bring it about that everyone had new reasons for loving their duties, their ruler, their country and their laws, and had a better sense of their good fortune in each land, in each government, in each position in which they find themselves, I would think myself the happiest of mortals.

p. 23 **b.** Corrected to *IV, 2,* from the original, mistaken reference to *IV, 1.*

c. *Cf.* Janet on Montesquieu:

On a reproché à Montesquieu la pensée et la méthode de son livre. Montesquieu, a-t-on dit, a plutôt étudié ce qui est que ce qui doit être ; il a des raisons pour tout ; tous les faits trouvent grâce à ses yeux, et quand il peut dire pourquoi une loi a été faite, il est satisfait, sans se demander si elle aurait dû l'être... Rien n'est plus injuste que ces imputations...

Lorsqu'on semble croire que Montesquieu est indifférent entre tous les faits qu'il expose, qu'il leur accorde à tous la même valeur, qu'il ne distingue pas le juste et l'injuste, on oublie les plus belles et les meilleures parties de son livre.
(Janet, *Histoire II:* 329, 332)

Montesquieu has been criticized because of his book's method and way of thinking. Montesquieu, it has been said, studied what is rather than what ought to be; he has an explanation for everything; all facts find favour in his eyes, and he is satisified when he can say why a law has been made, without asking if it should have been... These accusations are wholly unfair...

Anyone who appears to think that Montesquieu is indifferent between all the facts he sets out, that he gives them the same value, that he does not distinguish the just and the unjust, forgets the best and finest parts of his book.

p. 23 **d.** Corrected to *XV, 6*, from the original reference to *XV, 8*.

XV, 6 seems the obvious, *XV, 8* an inappropriate reference:

C'est là l'origine juste, et conforme à la raison, de ce droit d'esclavage très doux que l'on trouve dans quelques pays. (*L'Esprit des Lois*, XV, 6)	Here is the just origin, in conformity with reason, of the law of a very mild slavery that is found in some countries.

XV, 7 discusses the origin of a "cruel" slavery, in climates where arduous work is performed through fear and coercion. *XV, 8* goes on to conclude:

Il n'y a peut-être pas de climat sur la terre où l'on ne pût engager au travail des hommes libres. Parce que les lois étaient mal faites on a trouvé des hommes paresseux : parce que ces hommes étaient paresseux, on les a mis dans l'esclavage. (*L'Esprit des Lois*, XV, 8)	Perhaps there is no climate on earth where work could not be done by freemen. Because there were badly made laws it turned out there were lazy men: because these men were lazy, they were turned into slaves.

e. Corrected to *XXIV, 25, 26*, from the original, mistaken reference to *XXV, 25, 26* (no such chapters exist).

XXIV, 25, 26 discuss the difficulty of religion's transfer from one country to another, and so seem the chapters Durkheim had in mind.

p. 24 **a.** Corrected to *praecipere*, instead of the original text's *praecipue*. The correction is suggested by Cuvillier, p. 46, n. 12.

p. 26 **a.** Changed to *XXVI, 3-5*, from the original reference to *XXVI, 4, 5*. *XXVI, 3* discusses civil laws (including domestic laws) that are contrary to natural law, and *XXVI, 4-5* continue with the discussion.

p. 28 **a.** *Cf.* Janet, attacking the view that Montesquieu went along with and accepted whatever was the case:

Il semblerait, à entendre ces critiques, que Montesquieu fût de l'école de Machiavel, et	It would seem, according to these critics, that Montesquieu belonged to the school of

qu'à l'exemple du politique du XVe siècle, il ait élevé un monument à l'utile au détriment de la justice. Rien n'est plus injuste que ces imputations.
(Janet, *Histoire II:* 329)

Machiavelli and that, following the example of the politics of the 15th century, he erected a monument to the useful, at the expense of the just. These accusations are wholly unfair.

p. 29 **a.** The passage translated by Durkheim is:

Avant qu'il y eût des lois faites, il y avait des rapports de justice possibles. Dire qu'il n'y a rien de juste ni d'injuste que ce qu'ordonnent ou défendent les lois positives, c'est dire qu'avant qu'ont eût tracé de cercle, tous les rayons n'étaient pas égaux.
(*L'Esprit des Lois,* I, 1)

Before there existed established laws, there existed possible relations of justice. To say that there is nothing just or unjust except that which positive laws order or prohibit is to say that before a circle was drawn, its radii were not all equal.

b. Durkheim's italics.

c. The passage referred to and indirectly quoted by Durkheim is:

La loi, en général, est la raison humaine, en tant qu'elle gouverne tous les peuples de la terre ; et les lois politiques et civiles de chaque nation ne doivent être que les cas particuliers où s'applique cette raison humaine.
(*L'Esprit des Lois,* I, 3)

Law, in general, is human reason, inasmuch as it governs all the peoples of the earth; and the civil and political laws of each nation should be only particular cases in which this human reason is applied.

CHAPTER 3

p. 31 **a.** Here, *civitates* is translated as "states and societies", since Durkheim is going to argue that Montesquieu in fact classifies, not just the ways societies are governed, but societies themselves.

p. 31 **b.** Durkheim's reference corresponds with pp. 195-6 of the original, 1839 edition and of the identical 5th, 1893 edition. The passage is:

Il n'est que trop manifeste, en effet, que le projet fondamental de Montesquieu n'a été nullement réalisé dans l'ensemble de l'exécution de son travail, qui, malgré l'éminent mérite de certains details, ne s'écarte pas essentiellement de la nature commune des divers travaux antérieurs, et ne tarde point, à vrai dire, à revenir, comme ceux-ci, au type primitif du Traité d'Aristote, dont il n'a pu d'ailleurs aucunement égaler, en regard au temps, la rationelle composition.
(Comte, *Cours IV:* 195-6)

Indeed, it is only too obvious that Montesquieu's fundamental project was not at all realized in the execution of his work as a whole. This, though excellent in certain details, does not essentially depart from the nature common to various earlier works, and in fact soon returns, like them, to the original, basic type of Aristotle's Treatise – nor, relative to the time, could it in any way equal its rational structure and composition.

p. 32 **a.** *X, 8* in fact discusses the case of 18th century Genoa and its rule over Corsica.

V, 8 discusses Venice, but throughout its history (including Montesquieu's own time), without specific reference to the middle ages. This is generally the case with the many references to Venice in *The Spirit of the Laws.* Montesquieu also discusses Holland, Switzerland and the German free towns as examples of republics.

p. 33 **a.** This letter, written as if from Venice, begins:

Une des choses qui a le plus exercé ma curiosité en arrivant en Europe, c'est l'histoire et l'origine des républiques.

One of the things that most exercised my curiosity when I came to Europe was the origin and history of republics.

It concludes, in the passages Durkheim presumably had in mind:

César opprima la République romaine, et la soumit à un pouvoir arbitraire.

Caesar oppressed the Roman republic and subjected it to arbitrary power.

L'Europe gémit longtemps sous un gouvernement militaire et violent ; et la douceur romaine fut changée en une cruelle oppression.

Cependant une infinité de nations inconnues sortirent du Nord, se répandirent comme des torrents dans les provinces romaines ; et trouvant autant de facilité à faire des conquêtes qu'à exercer leurs pirateries, elles démembrèrent l'Empire et fondèrent des royaumes. Ces peuples étaient libres, et ils bornaient si fort l'autorité de leurs rois qu'ils n'étaient proprement que des chefs ou des généraux... Voilà le principe fondamental de tous ces États, qui se formèrent des débris de l'Empire romain.

(*Lettres persanes*, CXXXI)

For a long time, Europe groaned under a harsh military government, and Roman mildness was turned into a cruel oppression.

But innumerable, unknown nations then came out of the north, spread like a torrent over the Roman provinces, and finding it just as easy to make conquests as to engage in their piracies, dismembered the Empire and founded kingdoms. These peoples were free, and set such strict limits to the authority of their kings that they were really only chieftains or generals... This is the fundamental principle of all the states formed out of the remains of the Roman Empire.

p. 33 **b.** *XI, 11* in fact discusses the kings of the Greek heroic age, while *XI, 12* continues with the discussion in the case of Rome.

p. 34 **a.** The passages Durkheim alludes to and translates are:

[L'amour de la république, dans une démocratie, est celui de la démocratie ; l'amour de la démocratie est celui de l'égalité.

L'amour de la démocratie est encore l'amour de la frugalité.] Chacun devant y avoir le même bonheur et les

[Love of the republic, in a democracy, is for democracy; love of democracy is for equality.

Love of democracy is also love of frugalness.] Since each should have the same happiness and the same advantages, they should taste the same

même avantages, y doit goûter
les mêmes plaisirs, et former
les mêmes espérances ; chose
qu'on ne peut attendre que de
la frugalité générale.
(*L'Esprit des Lois,* V, 3)

pleasures and form the same
expectations – something that
can be envisaged as coming
about only from the general
frugalness.

p. 35 **a.** Durkheim presumably refers to the passage:

Comme l'égalité des fortunes
entretient la frugalité, la
frugalité maintient l'égalité des
fortunes. Ces choses, quoique
différentes, sont telles qu'elles
ne peuvent subsister l'une sans
l'autre ; chacune d'elles est la
cause et l'effet ; si l'une se
retire de la démocratie, l'autre
la suit toujours.

Just as equality of fortunes
supports frugalness, frugalness
sustains equality of fortunes.
These things, although different, are such that they cannot
continue to exist without one
another; they are each both
cause and effect; if, in a
democracy, one of them
disappears, the other always
follows.

But Montesquieu immediately goes on to argue:

Il est vrai que, lorsque la
démocratie est fondée sur le
commerce, il peu fort bien
arriver que des particuliers y
aient de grandes richesses, et
que les mœurs n'y soient pas
corrompues. C'est que l'esprit
de commerce entraîne avec soi
celui de frugalité, d'économie,
de modération, de travail, de
sagesse, de tranquillité, d'ordre et de règle. Ainsi, tandis
que cet esprit subsiste, les
richesses qu'il produit n'ont
aucun mauvais effet. Le mal
arrive, lorsque l'excès des

It is true that when democracy
is founded on commerce it can
very well happen that there are
individuals who have great
wealth, and yet that morals are
not corrupted. This is because
the spirit of commerce brings
with it a spirit of frugalness,
economy, moderation, hard
work, good sense, peaceful-
ness, order and rule. Then, as
long as this spirit continues to
exist, the wealth it produces
does not have any bad effect.
The trouble comes when ex-
cess of wealth destroys this

richesses détruit cet esprit de commerce ; on voit tout à coup naître les désordres de l'inégalité, qui ne s'étaient pas encore fait sentir.	spirit of commerce; one sees a birth, all at once, of disorders of inequality that had not made themselves felt before.

(*L'Esprit des Lois,* V, 6)

p. 35 **b.** *Quid* must be the subject of the singular verb, *efficiat,* and the plural *voluntates conspirantes* must be its object. So perhaps both the French translations misprint *ce qui* as *ce que:*

Il est facile de comprendre ce qui peut faire, dans une telle société, le concours de toutes les volontés.	It is easy to understand what, in such a society, can bring about the union of all wills.
Il est facile de comprendre ce que peut faire, dans une telle sociéte, le concours de toutes les volontés.	It is easy to understand what, in such a society, the union of all wills can bring about.
(Alengry: 431)	

Ce qui peut faire, dans une telle société, la volonté unanime de tous les citoyens, on le comprend facilement.	It is easy to understand what, in such a society, can bring about the united will of all citizens.
Ce que peut faire, dans une telle société, la volonté unanime de tous les citoyens, on le comprend facilement.	It is easy to imagine what the unanimous will of the citizens can accomplish in such a society.
(Cuvillier: 61)	(tr. Manheim: 28.)

p. 36 **a.** This involves an ambiguity, that Durkheim skips over, between the views that no one should be allowed (1) to do things outside of a fixed role they occupy, however they came to occupy it, versus (2) to change their occupancy of one fixed role for occupancy of another.

Montesquieu's views involve elements not just of (1) and, in a rigid division of labour, a *régime des fonctions,* but also of (2) and a *régime des castes.*

p. 37 **a.** Durkheim repeatedly uses the noun, *societas.* But it is only in this phrase, *sociale vinculum,* that he uses the adjective, *socialis.* The adjectival term he uses in its stead is *civilis,* as in *civilia facta.*

p. 38 **a.** Durkheim's italics.

p.39 **a.** Corrected to *principales,* misprinted in the thesis as *principes.*

b. Janet quotes passages from *The Spirit of the Laws,* III, 3 and 5.

Durkheim's anodyne reference to these covers up a fundamental disagreement with Janet. According to Durkheim, Montesquieu's criticisms in them of monarchy should not be thought to amount to a condemnation of it, and he also argues, later on, that Montesquieu prefers monarchy to a republic. According to Janet:

Montesquieu y compare la monarchie et la république ; et au ton satirique dont il parle de la première, à l'admiration avec laquelle il expose le principe de la seconde, il est impossible de ne pas voir en lui, à cette époque, un partisan de la république et un adversaire de la monarchie.

[quotations from III, 3 and 5]

Il est difficile de stigmatiser en termes plus forts les vices de la monarchie. Sans doute, Montesquieu atténuait cette satire en disant ensuite qu'à la place de la vertu la monarchie a pour ressort l'honneur, c'est-à-dire ce principe qui fait faire les bonnes actions, non parce qu'elles sont bonnes, mais parce qu'elles sont belles, et parce qu'on ne veut pas être méprisable à ses propres yeux. Sans doute, il

Montesquieu compares monarchy and the republic; from the satirical tone in which he talks of the first and the admiration with which he sets out the principle of the second, it is impossible not to view him, at this time, as a partisan of the republic and as an opponent of monarchy.

[quotations from III, 3 and 5]

It is difficult to pillory the vices of monarchy in stronger terms. No doubt Montesquieu toned down this satire in saying, later on, that in place of virtue monarchy has the motivational spring of honour – that is, the principle which brings about good actions, not because they are good, but because they are glorious and because one does not want to be contemptible in one's own eyes. No doubt he tried to talk

essayait de relever la monarchie dans deux chapitres éloquents, mais c'était surtout la monarchie des temps passés, car de son temps ce principe de l'honneur n'avait, disait-il, plus de force ; « on avait mis l'honneur en contradiction avec les honneurs, et l'on voyait des gens chargés d'infamie et de dignités. » Il n'est pas moins vrai cependant que Montesquieu partageait cette tendance générale de son temps, qui préférait théoriquement la république à la monarchie.

(Janet, *Histoire II:* 469-70)

up monarchy in two eloquent chapters, but it was above all the monarchy of past times, since, as he said, in his own time the principle of honour had lost its force; "honour has been set in opposition to honours, and men can be seen covered with infamy and with dignities" [*cf.* VIII, 7]. It is also no less true that Montesquieu shared the general tendency in his time, that in theory preferred a republic to monarchy.

p. 39 **c.** The next chapter begins:

Je me hâte, et je marche à grands pas, afin qu'on ne croie pas que je fasse une satire du gouvernement monarchique.

(*L'Esprit des Lois*, III, 6)

I quickly press on, in case it is thought that I satirize monarchical government.

p. 40 **a.** Corrected simply to *XIX,* from the original reference to *XIX, 2.*

XIX, as a whole, discusses "the general spirit, morals and manners" of different nations. *XIX, 2* is too limited and peculiar to seem the right reference.

Perhaps, in a printing error, "2" was switched around, so that in the reference in note 3, what should have been *XIX* became *XIX, 2,* while in note 5 what should have been *XXIII, 2 et sq.* just became *XXIII* – see note c, below.

b. Corrected to *XXIV-XXV,* from the original reference to *XXIV, 5.*

XXIV and *XXV* offer a general discussion of different religions; *XXIV, 5,* linking Catholicism with monarchy and Protestantism with a republic, again seems too limited to be the right reference.

p. 40 **c.** Corrected to *XXIII, 2 et sq.*, from the original reference to *XXIII*.
XXIII, 2-10 discuss the family and marriage; *XXIII* as a whole is concerned with population size.

d. *XVI* does discuss marriage, as Durkheim says, although its title in fact refers to "domestic slavery".

e. *XII, 18 et sq.* does involve a discussion of crime and punishment, though the topic's main discussion is in book *VI*.

p. 42 **a.** The objection Durkheim sets up (to knock down) is a paraphrase of Janet:

[L]a différence de la monarchie et du despotisme n'est pas aussi grande que le dit l'auteur. Car, dans la monarchie... le prince, excepté un très petit nombre de lois fondamentales, peut toujours changer les lois ; s'il ne les change pas, c'est qu'il ne le veut pas. Sa volonté est la supreme loi : c'est là le principe même du despotisme. (Janet, *Histoire II:* 345)	[T]he difference between monarchy and despotism is not as great as Montesquieu says. For, in monarchy..., except for a very small number of fundamental laws, the ruler can always change the laws; if he does not change them, it is because he does not want to. His will is the supreme law – the same principle as in despotism.

b. In fact, Janet does not argue that there has never been any instance, however "abnormal", of absolute, unfettered tyranny:

D'ailleurs, s'il n'est pas exact de dire que la monarchie soit nécessairement soumise à des lois fixes, est-il plus exact de dire que le despotisme n'est soumise absolument à aucune loi ? A qui fera-t-on croire que le gouvernement des Turcs, des Persans et des Chinois, soit absolument sans règle, sans frein, sans usages, sans	Moreover, if it is not exact to say that monarchy is necessarily subject to fixed laws, is it any more exact to say that despotism is absolutely not subject to any law? Who is going to believe that in the government of the Turks, of the Persians and of the Chinese there is an absolute lack of any rule, any brake,

quelque chose enfin qui limite la volonté arbitraire du prince ou de ses subordonnés ? Qu'une telle forme de gouvernement se rencontre par hasard, lorsqu'un Caracalla ou un Héliogabale occupe le trône, cela ne peut pas se nier ; mais que ce soit là une forme normale et vraiment essentielle de gouvernement parmi les hommes, c'est ce qui est contraire à la nature des choses.	any conventions and practices and in sum anything that limits the arbitrary will of the ruler or his subordinates? It is undeniable that such a form of government makes a chance appearance when a Caracalla or a Heliogabulus occupies the throne. But what is against the nature of things is that this is a normal, truly essential form of government among mankind.

(Janet, *Histoire II:* 345-6)

p. 43 **a.** Corrected to *ces pays..., tant de force...,* and *des lois,* misprinted in the thesis as *ce pays..., tant de forces...,* and *de lois.*

b. Corrected to *leur prince,* misprinted in the thesis as *le prince.*

c. The reference to the old having most authority should still be to *XVIII, 13.* It is the reference to love of freedom that is to *XVIII, 14.*

d. Corrected to *XVIII, 11,* from the original, mistaken *XVIII, 1.*

CHAPTER 4

p. 45 **a.** From the opening passage of *The Spirit of the Laws:*

Les lois, dans la signification la plus étendue, sont les rapports nécessaires qui dérivent de la nature des choses : et, dans ce sens, tous les êtres ont leurs lois.	Laws, understood in the most general way, are the necessary connexions which follow from the nature of things and, in this sense, all beings have their laws.

(*L'Esprit des Lois,* I, 1)

b. The reference corresponds with the original edition's p. 196. The passage is:

Après avoir reconnu, en principe général, la subordination nécessaire des phénomènes sociaux à d'invariables lois naturelles, on ne voit plus, dans le cours de l'ouvrage, que les faits politiques y soient, en réalité, nullement rapportés au moindre aperçu de ces lois fondamentales : et même la stérile accumulation de ces faits, indifféremment empruntés, souvent sans aucune critique vraiment philosophique, aux états de civilisation les plus opposés, paraît directement repousser toute idée d'un véritable enchaînement scientifique.

(Comte, *Cours IV:* 196)

After the recognition, as a general principle, that social phenomena are necessarily subject to invariable natural laws, all that is then evident, during the work, is that the political facts in it are in reality unrelated to any notion whatsoever of these fundamental laws. Even the sterile accumulation of these facts, taken just as readily, often without any genuine philosophical critique, from the most opposed states of civilization, seems a direct repudiation of the whole idea of a truly scientific sequence and connexion of things.

p. 46 **a.** The full passage, quoted in notes 1-3, reads:

[n. 2] Il est de la nature d'une république qu'elle n'ait qu'un petit territoire ; sans cela elle ne peut guère subsister. *[n. 3]* Dans une grande république, il y a de grandes fortunes, et par conséquent peu de modération dans les esprits : il y a de trop grands dépôts à mettre entre les mains d'un citoyen ; les intérêts se particularisent ; un homme sent d'abord qu'il peut être heureux, grand, glorieux, sans sa patrie ; et bientôt, qu'il peut être seul grand sur les ruines de sa patrie.

[n. 2] It is in the nature of a republic to have only a small territory; otherwise, it can hardly continue to exist. *[n. 3]* In a large republic, there are large fortunes, and as a result little moderation in outlook and character; the stores are too large to put in the hands of one citizen; interests become particularized; at first a man feels that he can be happy, great and glorious without his country, and soon that he can be great only on the ruins of his country.

Dans une grande république, le bien commun est sacrifié à mille considérations ; il est subordonné à des exceptions ; il dépend des accidents. *[n. 1]* Dans une petite, le bien public est mieux senti, mieux connu, plus près de chaque citoyen. (*L'Esprit des Lois,* VIII, 16)	In a large republic, the common good is sacrificed to a thousand considerations; it is subordinated to exceptions; it depends on accidents. *[n. 1]* In a small one, the public good is better felt, better known, and closer to each citizen.

p. 49   **a.** Corrected to *sur les sauvages,* misquoted in the thesis as *chez les sauvages.*

p. 50   **a.** Corrected to *IV, 6,* from the original, mistaken reference, which is to *IV, 34* (no such chapter exists).

b. The original passage, somewhat freely translated into Latin by Durkheim, is:

Fait pour vivre dans la société, il y pouvait oublier les autres ; les législateurs l'ont rendu à ses devoirs par les lois politiques et civiles. (*L'Esprit des Lois,* I, 1)	Formed to live in society, he may forget about other people; legislators have brought him back to his duties through political and civil laws.

p. 51   **a.** The important clause, *quibus tamen carere potest,* duly appears in the French translation by Cuvillier, p. 83, but is unaccountably left out in the English translation of this by Manheim, p. 41.

p. 55   **a.** The full passage is in fact:

Il y a cette différence [a] entre la nature du gouvernement et son principe, que sa nature est ce qui le fait être tel, et son principe ce qui le fait agir. L'une est sa structure particulière, et l'autre les passions humaines qui le font mouvoir.	There is this difference[a] between the nature of the government and its principle, that its nature is that which makes it what it is, its principle that which makes it act. One is its particular structure, the other the human passions which set it in motion.

a. Cette distinction est très importante, et j'en tirerai bien des conséquences ; elle est la clef d'une infinité de lois. (*L'Esprit des Lois,* III, 1)	**a.** This distinction is very important, and I shall draw many consequences from it; it is the key to an infinity of laws.

Perhaps Durkheim's selective quotation is to suggest that in Montesquieu's theory a society's "nature" in the sense of its structure is also its nature in the sense of its essence – defined as the properties of a thing which (1) contain, in themselves, all the others, and (2) determine the particular kind of thing it is. In that case, it would be a society's structure which both (1) contained, *inter alia,* its principle, and (2) determined the kind of society it was.

But whether or not this is in fact what Durkheim implies, it is a misinterpretation of Montesquieu's theory. Both a society's structure and its principle constitute, interactingly, its essence – though it is its principle which is, if anything, more important.

p. 55   **b.** The primary meaning of *adventicius* is "coming from without", "from outside sources", "external", "coming from abroad", "foreign". This is somewhat lost in the translation as *adventice* by Alengry, p. 448. It is completely lost in the translation as *accidentelle* by Cuvillier, p. 89 (cf. Manheim, p. 45).

In Latin dictionaries of Durkheim's time, a secondary meaning is given as "casual", "extraordinary", "accidental", and Durkheim's discussion links the two meanings – something again lost in Cuvillier's translation, which is completely unjustified. Indeed, its talk of causes that are "fortuitous and, as it were, accidental" destroys the point of the "as it were", in making it connect two terms that mean the same thing.

In the passage to which Durkheim refers, it is clear that Montesquieu has in mind something like "accidental and, as it were, external" causes that, coming from outside a republican or monarchical sociopolitical system, threaten to undermine it:

Le principe du gouvernement despotique se corrompt sans cesse, parce qu'il est corrompu par sa nature. Les autres	The principle of despotic government is continually corrupted, since it is corrupt by its nature. The other govern-

gouvernements périssent, parce que des accidents particuliers en violent le principe :
celui-ci périt par son vice
intérieur, lorsque quelques
causes accidentelles n'empêch-
ent point son principe de se
corrompre.

(L'Esprit des Lois, VIII, 10)

ments are destroyed because
particular accidents violate
their principle: this one is
destroyed by its internal vice
if accidental causes do not
prevent the corruption of its
principle.

p. 56 **a.** The reference to Zeller is to one of the best-known, established
authorities at the time on Greek philosophy. The passage is worth
quoting at some length, because of its importance for Durkheim's
interest in the linked issues of the normal versus the pathological, the
essential versus the contingent, and internalist versus externalist
("accidental") explanation:

[/p. 332] Ebendesshalb ist
aber der Umfang, in welchem
der Naturzweck sich verwirklicht, die Art und die Vollkom-
menheit, in welcher [/p. 333]
die Form zur Erscheinung
kommt, durch die Beschaffenheit dieser Stoffe, durch ihre
Fähigkeit zur Aufnahme und
Darstellung der Form bedingt,
und in demselben Mass, wie
es ihnen an dieser Fähigkeit
gebricht, werden sich theils
unvollkommene, von der rein-
en Form und dem eigentlich-
en Naturzweck abweichende
Bildungen, theils auch solche
Erzeugnisse ergeben, die über-
haupt keinem Zweck dienen,
sondern bei der Verwick-
lichung der Naturzwecke nur
nebenher, vermöge des Natur-

[/p. 332] For the same reason,
the extent to which Nature
can realise her end - the mode
and the perfection in which
[/p. 333] the Form manifests
itself - are conditioned by the
character of these materials:
that is, by their capacity for
receiving and exhibiting the
Form. Just in proportion as
this capacity is wanting, will
the formations be imperfect
and degenerate from their true
patterns and the proper
purposes of nature, or perhaps
we shall have productions
which serve no end at all,
but are developed incidentally
as the result of some natural
coherence and necessity, in
the course of the realisation
of Nature's purposes. We

zusammenhangs und seiner Nothwendigkeit, hervorgebracht werden. Wir werden später finden, wie tief dieser Punkt in Aristoteles' ganze Naturansicht eingreift, und vie viele Erscheinungen er aus dem Widerstreben des Stoffs gegen die Form herleitet. Dieselbe Beschaffenheit des Stofflichen ist es aber auch, von der Zufälligkeit in der Natur herrührt. Unter [/p. 334] dem Zufälligen versteht nämlich Aristoteles, welcher diesen Begriff zuerst genauer untersucht hat, im allgemeinem alles das, was einem Ding gleichsehr zukommen und nicht zukommen kann, was nicht in seinem Wesen enthalten und durch die Nothwendigkeit seines Wesens gesetzt ist., was daher weder nothwendig noch in der Regel stattfindet... [/p. 335] das Zufällige entsteht dadurch, dass eine freie oder unfreie Zweckthätigkeit durch die Einwirkung äusserer Umstände auf einen ihrem Zweck fremden Erfolg hingelenkt wird. Und da nun diese einwirkenden [/p.336] Umstände doch immer in der Beschaffenheit der materiellen Mittel, durch welche eine Zweckthätigkeit sich vollzieht,

shall hereafter have occasion to observe how deeply this view is rooted in Aristotle's whole theory of Nature, and how many phenomena he accounts for by the resistance of Matter to Form. Again the same property of Matter is also the source of all contingency in Nature. By [/p. 334] 'the contingent,' Aristotle, who was the first carefully to examine this conception, understands in general all that can equally well belong or not belong to a thing: that which is neither contained in its essence nor supported by the necessity of its being, and which accordingly is neither necessary nor normal... [/p. 335] A contingent or accidental event is caused by the diversion of free or compulsory purposeful action to results alien from its purpose through the influence of external circumstances. Now, since these disturbing [/p. 336] circumstances are always found in the nature of the material means by which ends are realised, and in the system of nature to which these means belong, Contingency, in Aristotle's

und in dem Naturzusammenhang, dem dieselben angehören, zu suchen sind, so liesse sich der Zufall im Sinn unseres Philosophen auch als Störung der Zweckthätigkeit durch die Mittelursachen definiren. Eine Zweckthätigkeit ist aber diejenige, in welcher das Wesen und der Begriff eines Gegenstandes sich verwirklicht; was nicht aus der Zweckthätigkeit hervorgeht, ist ein wesenloses, und Aristoteles sagt desshalb, das Zufällige stehe dem Nichtseienden nahe. Dass ein solches auch nicht Gegenstand der Wissenschaft sein kann, braucht nach allem, was früher über die Aufgabe des Wissens bemerkt wurde, kaum ausdrücklich gesagt zu werden.
(Zeller, *Die Philosophie der Griechen II, 2:* 332-6)

sense, may be defined as the disturbance by intermediate causes of an activity directed to a purpose. But activity in obedience to a purpose is that by which the essence or conception of an object is realised. That which does not proceed from it is unessential; and therefore Aristotle says that the contingent borders on the non-existent. After what has already been said about the nature of Knowledge, it scarcely needs, therefore, to be explicitly stated that such a principle as Contingency can be no object of Science.

(tr. Costelloe & Muirhead, I: 360-5)

p. 56 **b.** Corrected to *XIV, 6,* from the original, mistaken reference, which is to *XIV, 16* (no such chapter exists).

c. Corrected to *XIV, 15,* from the original, mistaken reference, which is to *XV, 15.*

CHAPTER 5

p. 60 **a.** Corrected to *societatum leges* ("laws of societies"), from the original text's *legum societates* ("societies of laws"). The phrase is in fact translated as "laws of society" by Alengry, p. 453. But the correction is pointed out by Cuvillier, p. 97, n. 1.

p. 61 **a.** Durkheim's italics.

p.61   **b.** References corrected to Books VI and VII, from the original, mistaken references to Books V and VI, and the titles have also been corrected, as indicated in the square brackets.

p. 63   **a.** The passage from Bacon is:

Subtilitas naturae subtilitatem sensus et intellectus multis partibus superat. (Bacon, *Novum Organum:* Aphorismi de interpretatione naturae et regno hominis, Aphorismus X)	The subtlety of nature exceeds by many times the subtlety of the senses and understanding. (Bacon, *New Organon:* Aphorisms on nature's interpretation and the kingdom of man, Aphorism X)

p. 68   **a.** Corrected to *non nullo alio superius* ("superior to any other"), from the original text's *nullo alio superius esse* ("superior to no other").

Non nihil ("not nothing" = "something"), *non nullus* ("not none" = "any"), etc., are common Latin constructions. The passage is straightforward and Durkheim makes complete sense if it is assumed that, by error, a *non* has been left out.

He makes little or no sense if this is not assumed – as can be seen from the struggles and distortions of the translations both by Alengry, p. 459, and by Cuvillier, p. 107 (*cf.* Manheim p.59).

b. In going on to complain that Montesquieu "does not realize that the nature of societies contains opposites, which struggle with one another", Durkheim might be thought somewhat selective and misleading, since the passage from which he quotes concludes, a few lines later:

Souvent les États fleurissent plus dans le passage insensible d'une constitution à une autre, qu'ils ne le faisaient dans l'une ou l'autre de ces constitutions. C'est pour lors que tous les ressorts du gouvernement sont tendus ; que tous les citoyens	States are often more flourishing in the imperceptible shift from one constitution to another than they are under either of these constitutions. It is at this time that all the springs of government are stretched: that all citizens have

ont des prétentions ; qu'on s'attaque ou qu'on se caresse ; et qu'il y a une noble émulation entre ceux qui défendent la constitution qui décline, et ceux qui mettent en avant celle qui prévaut.
(*L'Esprit des Lois,* XI, 13)

claims; that one makes enemies or friends; and that there is a noble rivalry between those who defend the constitution which is in decline and those who campaign for the one which wins out.

CONCLUSION

p. 71 **a.** Corrected to *397-399,* from the original mistaken reference to *317-319.* The passage begins and concludes:

Mais un commentaire de l'*Esprit des lois* devrait-il être une perpétuelle critique de l'*Esprit des lois* ? Je voudrais que quelqu'un fît voir avec détail la beauté du livre de Montesquieu, la vaste étendue de l'obscurité du sujet choisi par lui et la force avec laquelle il s'en rendu maître, les difficultés de la matière et le succès de l'entreprise...

Il fallait donc à la fois examiner ces rapports isolément et les considérer ensemble. Que si l'on se fait une idée juste de toute cette complication, peut-être sera-t-on moins frappé de ce qui manque au livre de Montesquieu ; peut-être admirera-t-on davantage la belle lumière qu'il a jetée sur un sujet si confus, et l'on ne s'étonnera point de cette fière parole de

But must a commentary on *The Spirit of the Laws* be a perpetual criticism of *The Spirit of the Laws*? I wish someone would build up a painstaking picture of the beauty of Montesquieu's work, the vastness and obscurity of the subject tackled by him and the force with which he mastered it, the difficulties of the material and the undertaking's success...

So it is necessary both to examine these relationships each on their own and to consider them as a whole. With understanding of the complexity of all this, one might be less struck by what is lacking in Montesquieu's book and more appreciative of the marvellous light he shed on so confused a subject, and would not be thrown by the proud

sa préface : « Quand j'ai découvert mes principes, tout ce que je cherchais est venu à moi. » En parlant ainsi, il se faisait sans doute illusion; et l'on peut trouver que ses principes sont loin d'avoir la portée et l'étendue qu'il leur prête ; lui-même les oublie souvent. Il n'en est pas moins le premier qui ait appliqué l'esprit scientifique, l'esprit moderne aux faits politiques et sociaux. Il est au moins le Descartes, s'il n'est pas le Newton de la politique.
(Janet, *Histoire II:* 397-9)

talk, in the preface: "Once I discovered my principles, everything I had been looking for came to me". No doubt, in speaking in this way, he deluded himself; it may be thought that his principles do not have anything like the range and impact he attributed to them; he himself often forgot them. He is, even so, the first to have applied the modern, scientific spirit to social and political facts. He is at least the Descartes, if he is not the Newton, of politics.

p. 71 **b.** Durkheim's reference is to the whole of Comte's discussion of Montesquieu; it corresponds with the original edition's pp. 193-201.

p. 73 **a.** There is no problem with Alengry's translation, p. 462 (*il ne semble pas possible...*). But in Cuvillier's, *ne semble pas pouvoir* is misprinted as *me semble pas pouvoir* – then translated by Manheim in a way that attributes to Durkheim the very view he is attacking:

Celle-ci est si mobile, si diverse et si riche de formes variées qu'elle me semble pas pouvoir se ramener à des lois déterminées et immuables.
(Cuvillier: 111-12)

...which is so mobile, diversified, and rich in forms that to my mind it cannot be reduced to fixed and immutable laws.

(tr. Manheim: 63)

p.74 **a.** At the end of the thesis there is an inscription:

Vidi ac perlegi: Lutetiae Parisiorum, in Sorbona, a. d. X. Kal. dec. ann. MD CCCXCII. Facultatis Litterarum in Academia Parisiensi Decanus, A. Himly.

Seen and read: Paris, the Sorbonne, 22nd November 1892. Dean of the Faculty of Arts, University of Paris, A. Himly.

On Taine

p. 75 **a.** This is an untitled piece that Durkheim contributed, at the invitation of the editor, to: Quelques opinions sur l'œuvre de H. Taine, *Revue blanche,* 13 (101) 1897: 263-295.

Other contributors included Maurice Barrès (266-268), Emile Boutroux (274-275) and Gabriel Tarde (284-286). Durkheim's contribution (287-291) is not only the longest, but, arguably, the most thoughtful and the most interesting. It is reprinted in Durkheim *Textes I:* 171-177, and an earlier version of the translation appeared in *Durkheimian Studies / Etudes Durkheimiennes,* n.s. 1, 1995: 9-15.

p. 81 **a.** Corrected to *en faire l'étude du point de vue de la science,* from the original text's *en faire la science du point de vue.* The correction is suggested by V. Karady, in *Textes I:* 176, editorial note.

b. The allusion is to *The Disciple,* a novel published in 1889 by Paul Bourget, a traditionalist, Catholic writer. The hero decides to put into practice the scientific, deterministic doctrines of a philosopher clearly identifiable as Taine, and, after disastrous consequences all round, returns to prayer, mystery and religion This is explained in a note, providing further background, by Dominique Merllié, *Durkheimian Studies / Etudes Durkheimiennes,* n.s. 2, 1996: 31-32.

BIBLIOGRAPHY

References to Durkheim follow the dating–enumeration system developed by Steven Lukes and W. S. F. Pickering.

Main texts

Durkheim. 1892a. *Quid Secundatus politicae scientiae instituendae contulerit.* Bordeaux: Gounouilhou.

— 1937b. Alengry's translation. Montesquieu: sa part dans la fondation des sciences politiques et de la science des sociétés. *Revue d'histoire politique et constitutionelle,* I: 405-463.

— 1953a. Cuvillier's translation. La contribution de Montesquieu à la constitution de la science sociale. In *Montesquieu et Rousseau, précurseurs de la sociologie.* Paris: Marcel Rivière. 25-113.

— 1960b. Manheim's translation of Cuvillier. *Montesquieu and Rousseau: forerunners of sociology.* Ann Arbor, Mich.: University of Michigan Press.

Montesquieu. [1748] 1758. *De l'esprit des loix.* Reproduced in: 1950. *Œuvres complètes de Montesquieu,* vol. I, published under the direction of A. Masson. Paris: Nagel.

— 1876-1878. *De l'esprit des lois.* In *Œuvres complétes de Montesquieu,* vols. III-VI, edited by E. Laboulaye. Paris: Garnier.

— 1973. *De l'esprit des lois* [2 volumes], edited by R. Derathé. Paris: Garnier.

Other works

Alengry, F. 1900. *Essai historique et critique sur la sociologie chez Auguste Comte.* Paris: Alcan.

Althusser, L. 1959. *Montesquieu, la politique et l'histoire.* Paris: Presses Universitaires de France.

Archambault, P. n. d. *Montesquieu. Choix de textes et introduction.* Paris: Louis-Michaud.

Aristotle (F. Susemihl & R. D. Hicks, eds.) 1894. *The Politics of Aristotle: a revised text with introduction, analysis and commentary.* London: Macmillan.

Aron, R. 1967. *Les étapes de la pensée sociologique.* Paris: Gallimard.

Bacon, F. (T. Fowler, ed.) 1889. *Novum Organum.* Oxford: Clarendon Press.

Benrekassa, G. 1987. *Montesquieu, la liberté et l'histoire*. Paris: Le Livre de Poche.

Beyer, C. 1982. *Nature et valeur dans la philosophie de Montesquieu: analyse méthodique de la notion de rapport dans "L'Esprit des Lois"*. Paris: Klincksieck.

Brethe de la Gressaye, J. 1950. Introduction to *Montesquieu. De l'esprit des loix,* vol. I. Paris: Société des Belles Lettres. vii-cxxx.

Brunschvicg, L. 1927. *Le Progès de la conscience dans la philosophie occidentale* [2 volumes]. Paris: Alcan.

Caillois, R. 1949. Introduction to *Montesquieu. Œuvres complètes,* vol. I. Paris: Gallimard. ix-xl.

Comte, A. 1839. *Cours de philosophie positive*, vol. IV. Paris: Bachelier. Reprinted in: 1893. *Cours de philosophie positive*, vol. IV. Paris: Au Siège de la Société Positiviste. Reproduced in: 1969. *Œuvres d'Auguste Comte*, vol. IV. Paris: Anthropos.

Constant, B. [1819] 1980. De la liberté des anciens comparée à celle des modernes. In *De la liberté chez les modernes*. Paris: Le Livre de Poche.

Cotta. S. 1953. *Montesquieu e la scienza sociale*. Turin: Ramella.

Davy, G. 1939. Sur la méthode de Montesquieu. *Revue de métaphysique et de morale*, XLVI: 571-586.

— 1949. Montesquieu et la science politique. In *IIe Centenaire de l'Esprit des lois*. Bordeaux: Delmas. 127-171.

Dedieu, J. 1913. *Montesquieu*. Paris: Alcan.

Durkheim, E. 1885a. Review of Schaeffle. *Revue philosophique*, XIX: 84-101. Reprinted in: 1975b. *Textes I*: 355-377.

— [1893b] 1902b. *La Division du travail social*, 2nd edn. Paris: Alcan.

— [1895a/1901c] 1947a. *Les règles de la méthode sociologique*, 2nd edn. Paris: Presses Universitaires de France.

— 1897a. *Le suicide: étude de sociologie*. Paris: Alcan.

— 1897f. Contribution to: Quelques opinions sur l'œuvre de H. Taine. *Revue blanche*, 13: 287-291.

— 1925a. *L'éducation morale*. Paris: Alcan.

— 1950a. *Leçons de sociologie*. Paris: Presses Universitaires de France.

— 1975b. *Textes* [3 volumes], edited by V.Karady. Paris: Editions de Minuit.

Faguet, E. 1890. *Le dix-huitième siècle.* Paris: Lecène & Oudin.

Ferguson, A. [1767] 1967. *An Essay on the History of Civil Society,* edited, with an introduction, by D. Forbes. Edinburgh: Edinburgh University Press.

Flint, R. 1874. *The Philosophy of History in France and Germany.* Edinburgh: Blackwood.

Fraisse, L. 1989. De l'imitation à l'organicisme: Montesquieu à la lumière des sociologues en 1880. *Revue d'histoire littéraire de la France,* 89: 195-219.

Gentile, F. 1975. Montesquieu philosophe et sociologue. In P. Dupouy, F. Gentile and P. Grosclaude, *Etudes sur Montesquieu, philosophie sociale et politique.* Paris: L'Académie Montesquieu. 31-53.

Goyard-Fabre, S. 1993. *Montesquieu: la nature, les lois, la liberté.* Paris: Presses Universitaires de France.

Gurvitch, G. 1939. La sociologie juridique de Montesquieu. *Revue de métaphysique et de morale,* XLVI: 611-626.

Hémon, F. n. d. *Cours de littérature, XV: Montesquieu.* Paris: Delagrave.

Hubert, R. 1939. La notion du devenir historique dans la philosophie de Montesquieu. *Revue de métaphysique et de morale,* XLVI: 587-640.

Janet, P. 1858. *Histoire de la philosophie morale et politique dans l'antiquité et les temps modernes* [2 volumes]. Paris: Ladrange.

— 1872. *Histoire de la science politique dans ses rapports avec la morale* [2 volumes], 2nd edn. Paris: Ladrange. (A revised and retitled edition of Janet 1858).

— 1887. *Histoire de la science politique, etc.,* 3rd edn. Paris: Alcan.

— 1913. *Histoire de la science politique, etc.,* 4th edn. Paris: Alcan.

Jones, R. A. 1994. Ambivalent Cartesians: Durkheim, Montesquieu and Method. *American Journal of Sociology,* 100: 1-39.

Laboulaye, E. 1876. Introduction to *l'Esprit des lois, Œuvres complètes de Montesquieu,* vol. III. Paris: Garnier. i-lxix.

Meek, R. 1976. *Social Science & the Ignoble Savage.* Cambridge: Cambridge University Press.

Montesquieu, C. S. de. [1721] 1758. *Lettres persanes.* Reproduced in: 1950. *Œuvres complétes de Montesquieu,* vol. I. Paris: Nagel.

— [1734] 1758. *Considérations sur les causes de la grandeur et de*

la décadence des Romains. Reproduced in: 1950. *Œuvres complétes de Montesquieu*, vol. I. Paris: Nagel.

— [1750] 1758. *Défense de l'Esprit des lois*. Reproduced in: 1950. *Œuvres complètes de Montesquieu*, vol. I. Paris: Nagel.

Rosso, C. 1971. *Montesquieu moraliste: des lois au bonheur*. Paris: Ducros.

Sainte-Beuve, C-A. 1853. Montesquieu. *Causeries du lundi*, VII: 33-66.

Schmaus, W. 1995. Explanation and essence in *The Rules of Sociological Method* and *The Division of Labor in Society*. *Sociological Perspectives*, 38: 57-75.

Shackleton, R. 1961. *Montesquieu, A Critical Biography*. Oxford: Oxford University Press.

Sorel, A. 1887. *Montesquieu*. Paris: Hachette.

Steadman Jones, S. 1996. What does Durkheim mean by "thing"? *Durkheimian Studies / Etudes Durkheimiennes*, n.s. 2: 43-60.

Taine, H. 1877. *Les origines de la France contemporaine*, vol. I, *L'ancien régime*. Paris: Hachette.

Tocqueville, A. [1835-40] 1961. *De la démocratie en Amérique*. Paris: Gallimard.

Vernière, P. 1977. *Montesquieu et l'Esprit des lois ou la raison impure*. Paris: Société d'Edition d'Enseignement Supérieur.

Waddicor, M. 1970. *Montesquieu and the Philosophy of Natural Law*. The Hague: Nijhoff.

Watts Miller, W. 1993. Durkheim's Montesquieu. *British Journal of Sociology*, 44: 693-712.

— 1996. *Durkheim, morals and modernity*. London: UCL Press.

— 1997. Liberté de la volonté et science sociale. In C-H. Cuin, ed., *La méthode durkheimienne d'un siècle à l'autre. Lectures actuelles des Règles de la méthode sociologique*. Paris: Presses Universitaires de France. 223-235.

Zeller, E. 1875. *Philosophie der Griechen*, vol. II, Pt. 2, 3rd edn. Leipzig: Fues. Costelloe & Muirhead translation: 1897. *Aristotle and the Earlier Peripatetics*. London: Longmans, Green.

Zévort, E. 1887. *Montesquieu*. Paris: Lecène & Oudin.

www.ingramcontent.com/pod-product-compliance
Lightning Source LLC
Chambersburg PA
CBHW060039030426
42334CB00019B/2395